D0835941

THE BIG BOOK OF

BODILY FUNCTIONS

THE BIG BOOK OF
BODILY FUNCTIONS

With an Introduction by
Jonathon Green

Cartoons by Dan Pearce

CASSELL&CO

Cassell & Co
Wellington House, 125 Strand, London WC2R 0BB

First published in 2001

ISBN 0-304-35743-X

Distributed in the United States by Sterling Publishing Co. Inc.
387 Park Avenue South, New York, NY 10016–8810

Design by Gwyn Lewis

Printed in Great Britain by Mackays of Chatham, Kent

contents

introduction

'Form ever follows function.' *Louis Sullivan*

So this is it, then, the final curtain, the famous last words, the *dernier cri*, the bottom (for how can I resist the pun in this linguistic company) line. The terminal volume of a trilogy that may not stand over-acute comparison with such magna opera as Aeschylus' *Oresteia*, Shakespeare's *Henry VI* or Schiller's *Wallenstein*, but which has a certain hedonistic, if unassailably down-market, kinship with that ever-popular, if oft excoriated triumvirate of sex and drugs and rock 'n' roll: the 'Big Books' of first 'Filth', then 'Being Rude' and now 'Bodily Functions'. If a certain thematic overlap seems visible, then my apologies: such is the linguistic taxonomy on offer. All three collections have come from the pages of *Cassell's Dictionary of Slang*. Together they comprise around 15,000 words and phrases. A plenitude, some may say, even an excess, but as I write that leaves a further 72,000 in the still-expanding database, a fact that if nothing else, must surely prove that slang, despite the vocabularies it offers here, isn't merely a seedy agglomeration of 'dirty words'.

The vocabulary that follows, however, does tend quite literally to scatologia: the bodily functions it illumines are on the whole not so enthusiastically itemised in 'polite society'. If all human life is here, it is that area epitomized by the dictum that '*inter faeces et urinam creavit ille nos*' and that life is nasty and brutish, although for some reason the short (and indeed the long and tall) seem to have escaped this collection, for all that slang does indeed deal with such individuals in due process.

Defecation, urination, expectoration, ejaculation, inebriation, inanition, impregnation and menstruation are all on offer. Only copulation and masturbation have been excluded; for that wide-ranging lexicon I recommend a re-perusal of *The Big Book of Filth*. We have death, depression and drunkenness; for those who like to give their urino-genital organs a 'special' name, well, here are some more, albeit less congratulatory than the personally bestowed. In addition there is the whole sticky range of fluids; blood, semen, smegma, vomit and the rest.

Writing the introduction to *The Big Book of Being Rude* I was at pains to explain the presence of so many personally, religiously, ethnically and nationally derogatory terms. The book did, as I recall, receive one complaint (yes, it was from a clergyman) but that appeared to refer to some tired and jadedly obscene sexual slang. Just as the dedicated moralist seems so regularly to condone violence while running terrified from sex, so are the 'dirty' words apparently more frightening than those that might hurt an individual. And the messenger, of course, is as condemned as the message.

Surprisingly, since I had expected it, the proponents of linguistic 'P.C.' remained otherwise occupied. Nor should this small volume, I would suggest, over-perturb those who would eschew personal abuse, since what lies in store is common to all – race, religion and skin-tone notwithstanding. As it was once averred, 'Celia shits', and Celia, not to mention her literary 'other half' Strephon, do a great deal more that seems best, or at least most widely, described by the dictionaries of slang. But neither their gender nor their ethnicity have the slightest bearing.

Having suggested that slang does not deserve its dismissal as nothing more than a respository of 'dirty words', how then to justify the presence of quite so many here? One returns as ever to the realm of the apposite. Slang, as I would define it, is a 'counter-language', existing, if the image is feasible, both in parallel to the standard and simultaneously in opposition to it. The terms for vomiting, for being drunk, for various bodily fluids, are limited if one searches only in a standard English dictionary. Yet their very intimacy, their inescapable role in the human condition, means that they are bound to colonize a more extensive selection for use in our informal vocabularies. Just as slang has always offered the many synonyms for sexual intercourse or for masturbation (activities that despite social changes are still seen, linguistically at least, as taboo) it can provide those for defecation, ejaculation and all the other bodily forms and functions displayed within these pages.

The function of language, declared the celebrated anthropologist Bronislaw Malinowski, is not to express thought [but] to play an active pragmatic part in human behaviour. What you have here is the language of function. You can't be more behavioural than that.

Jonathon Green

abbreviations

abbr.	abbreviation
Anglo-Ind.	Anglo-Indian
Aus.	Australia, Australian
Bdos	Barbados, Barbadian
c.	*circa* (around)
Can.	Canada, Canadian
dial.	dialect, dialectal
esp.	especially
euph.	euphemism, euphemistic
Guyn.	Guyana, Guyanese
joc.	jocular
juv.	juvenile
Ling. Fr.	Lingua Franca
milit.	military
mispron.	mispronunciation
N.Z.	New Zealand
naut.	nautical
orig.	originally
pron.	pronunciation
rhy. sl.	rhyming slang
Scot.	Scotland, Scots, Scottish
SE	Standard English
sl.	slang
Und.	Underworld
usu.	usually
W.I.	West Indies

How to Enjoy
The Big Book of Bodily Functions

The Big Book of Bodily Functions presents slang words relating to the body, its functions and its fluids under a variety of categories and headings. Each word or phrase is followed by a date in square brackets, [18C], [19C], [late 18C–early 19C] and so on, indicating the period of usage of the word or phrase in question. The '+' sign indicates that the term is still in use, as does the date [2000s] which indicates a recent and current expression.

The round brackets that follow the square brackets contain a range of different types of additional information, including usage labels indicating the geographical usage of the word, e.g. (US) or the social/cultural usage, e.g. (US campus). Where necessary the round brackets also include glosses or etymological explanations for some of the more baffling expressions.

ANAL FUNCTIONS

THE ACT OF DEFECATION

big hit [1920s+] (Aus.; rhy. sl.)

b.m. [1960s+] (*bowel movement*)

crap [late 19C+]

crash [20C] (Aus.)

dump [1940s+] (orig. US)

grot [1940s+] (N.Z.)

grunties [1990s]

Irish shave [20C]

load off one's behind [1920s+]

load off one's mind [1920s+]

number two/number twos [1930s+] (mainly juv.)

shit [early 18C+]

shite [late 19C+]

○○○○○○○○○○○○○○○○○○○○○○○○○○○○○○○○○○
Defecatory specialities
cockney's luxury [late 19C–1950s] (breakfast in
  bed and use of the pot for defecation, rather
  than leaving the warm house for a trip to the
  outdoor privy)

kangaroo shit [1920s+] (Aus.; defecation in a
  squatting position)

○○○○○○○○○○○○○○○○○○○○○○○○○○○○○○○○○○

TO DEFECATE

bog [16C]

bury a quaker [18C–19C] (*quaker* = a long hard piece of excrement)

choke a darkie [1960s+] (Aus.)

chuck a turd [19C+]

cope [20C] (Ulster)

cramber [20C]

crap [late 19C+]

crimp one off [1990s+]

curl one off [1990s+]

despatch one's cargo [1910s–20s]

do a job [late 19C+]

do a jobbie [late 19C+]

do a job for oneself [20C]

do a rear/have a rear [20C] (orig. campus)

do a shit [mid-19C+]

do big jobs [20C] (orig. US juv.)

do one's business [late 19C+]

do one's dirty [1970s] (US)

do one's duty [20C]

drop one's bundle [late 19C+]

drop one's load [mid-19C+]

drown the brown turtle [1990s]

drown the brown turtle

dump [1950s–60s]

go and sing 'sweet violets' [20C] (euph.)

go grunts [1960s]

go to quat [19C]

grow a tail [1990s]

grunt [1930s–40s]

have a clear-out [1920s+]

18 ANAL FUNCTIONS

heave a Havana [1990s]

hockie/hockey/hocky [19C+]

kak [1960s+]

kangaroo it [1920s+] (Aus.; to defecate in a squatting position)

lay a cable [1990s]

lay a log [1970s+]

let go a black bass [1990s]

lump [1970s+]

open the bomb-bay doors [1990s]

park a darkie [1990s]

park one's breakfast [1990s]

ooooooooooooooooooooooooooooooooo
Defecation imminent ...

bake it [late 19C+] (to refrain from visiting the
  lavatory, however desperate the need)

sit on a horse's head/sit on an elephant
  [1990s] (to be about to pass a very large stool)

turtlehead [1990s] (to be urgently in need of
  defecation; i.e. the stool is already protruding
  from the anus)

touch cloth [1990s] (i.e. the stool is touching
  one's underwear)

touch socks [1990s] (i.e. the stool has emerged
  and has reached one's socks)

ooooooooooooooooooooooooooooooooo

park one's fudge [1990s]

pinch a loaf [1990s]

pinch one off [1990s]

piss backwards [late 19C–1900s]

poo [1950s+]

poop [early 18C+]

poo-poo [1960s+]

post a letter [20C]

rake one's cage out [1990s]

scutter [1970s+] (Irish *sciodar*, diarrhoea)

set a black bass free [1990s]

○○○○○○○○○○○○○○○○○○○○○○○○○○○○○○○○○○
... Defecation difficult

abort [1960s] (US gay; to defecate immediately
  following anal intercourse)

build a log cabin [1990s] (orig. US campus; to
  pass a large stool)

dump one's change [1980s+] (US Black/drugs; to
  excrete bags of drugs after swallowing them
  when facing a police search)

preeze [mid–late 19C] (to make ineffectual,
  straining efforts to defecate or urinate)

shit a brick [late 19C+] (to defecate after a
  lengthy period of constipation)

○○○○○○○○○○○○○○○○○○○○○○○○○○○○○○○○○○

Al fresco

do an agricultural [20C]

do a rural [20C]

go for a walk with a spade [20C]

sink the Bismarck [1990s] (to pass a large stool)

squat [1930s+]

squeeze (one's head) [20C]

strain some potatoes [1990s]

strangle a darkie [1960s+] (Aus.)

take a crap [late 19C+]

take a dump [1940s+]

take a shit [20C]

take a squat [1930s+]

take the kids to the pool [1990s]

tush [1910s] (W.I.)

EXCREMENT

Admiral Browning [20C] (orig. naut.)

big jobs [20C] (juv.)

body wax [20C]

boom-boom [1960s+] (US juv.)

To shit oneself

bog [16C]

brown trout [20C] (prison; to throw
excrement or urine over another
prisoner)

commit oneself [20C] (Ulster)

crap oneself [late 19C+]

fudge [1980s+] (US)

shit oneself [1960s+]

●●●●●●●●●●●●●●●●●●●●●●●●●●●●●●●●●●●

brunswick [19C] (US)

business [mid-19C+]

ca-ca [18C+] (Latin *cacare*, to defecate)

cack [late 19C+]

cacky [late 19C+]

crap [late 19C+]

daff [1950s+] (Irish)

danna [late 18C–mid-19C]

dookey/dooky/dookie [1960s+]

dukie [1960s+]

dooty [1960s+] (US juv.)

dust [19C]

fudge [1970s+] (US)

gerry [16C]

gick [1990s+] (Irish)

grunt [1940s+] (US)

hockey/hockie/hocky [19C+]

honey [1920s+] (US)

honeydew [1920s+] (US)

hooey [1980s+] (US)

jam [1970s] (US gay)

jib jobs [1990s]

kak [18C+] (Latin *cacare*, to defecate)

honey

Soft and sticky

clart [1970s+] (sticky excrement)

poot [1950s+] (US, usu. juv.; soft excrement)

sozzle [20C] (dial. *sossle*, a liquid mess)

ooooooooooooooooooooooooooooooooooo

keech [1970s+]

mierda [1990s] (Spanish, 'shit')

mud [1990]

owl-dung [mid-19C+] (US)

owl-feathers [mid-19C+] (US)

owl-milk [mid-19C+] (US)

owl-shit [mid-19C+] (US)

poep [1960s+] (S. Afr.; Afrikaans, 'fart')

poo [1950s+] (usu. juv.)

poop [mid-18C+]

poopie-plops [1950s+] (juv.)

poo-poo [1960s+]

puckey/pucky [1950s+]

scharn [20C]

scutter [1970s+] (Irish)

shaving cream [1950s] (US)

shit [early 18C+]

shite [late 19C+]

Excrement and excretion in rhyming slang: part 1

Rhyming with 'shit'

big hit [1920s+] (Aus.)

bob and hit [19C]

Brad Pitt [1980s+]

Eartha Kitt [1950s+]

Edgar Britt [1960s+]

florin [1990s] (playing on 'two-bob bit')

hard hit [1970s]

tomtit [1940s+]

two-bob bit [20C]

William (Pitt) [1950s+]

ooooooooooooooooooooooooooooooooooooooo

siege [16C]

smoky joe [1990s] (from the fumes it exudes)

squat [1970s+] (US)

taunty [mid-19C+] (Cheshire dial.)

toot [1960s+]

tush [1940s] (W.I.)

yackum [late 19C]

TURDS

alley apple [1950s–60s] (US)

black bass [1990s]

brownie [1970s]

brown trout [1990s]

bum cigar [1990s]

bum spud [1990s]

choad [1980s+]

copper bolts [20C]

curl [1990s]

doober [1970s+]

dreck [1920s+] (German)

○○○○○○○○○○○○○○○○○○○○○○○○○○○○○○○○

Excrement and excretion in rhyming slang: part 2

Rhyming with 'crap'

game of nap [20C]

horse and trap [20C]

macaroni [1970s+] ('pony')

man-trap [late 19C–1900s]

pony [late 19C+] (i.e. *pony* and trap)

Sheffield handicap [20C]

○○○○○○○○○○○○○○○○○○○○○○○○○○○○○○○○

Sex and shitting

cinnamon stick [1940s–60s] (gay; the faeces-stained penis after anal intercourse)

dumper [1960s+] (a sexual deviant with an obsession with excrement and defecation, as encountered by prostitutes)

facial [1970s+] (a prostitute's client who likes the prostitute to sit on his face, sometimes after she has inserted a suppository)

felch queen [1950s] (a gay man who is stimulated by faecal matter)

get some duke [1970s+] (to have someone's fist pushed into one's anus; *dukie* = excrement)

hot dog [20C] (to engage in coprophagy)

kaka queen [1950s–60s] (gay; one whose sexual preferences involve excrement, a coprophage)

scat [1960s+] (defecation for sexual purposes; *scat*ology)

●●●●●●●●●●●●●●●●●●●●●●●●●●●●●●●●●●●●

dump [1940s+] (orig. US)

fudge baby [1990s]

grot [1940s+] (N.Z.)

jere [16C] (UK Und.; Romani *jeer*, excrement)

jobbie [mid-19C+] (orig. Scot.)

bum cigar

○○○○○○○○○○○○○○○○○○○○○○○○○○○○○○○○○○○○

The turd in rhyming slang

Henry the Third [1950s+]

lemon curd [1960s+]

my word [20C]

Richard (the Third) [late 19C+]

William the Third [1960s–70s] (Aus.)

○○○○○○○○○○○○○○○○○○○○○○○○○○○○○○○○○○○○

jobby [mid-19C+] (orig. Scot.)

kuka [20C] (W.I.; 'ca-ca')

kungse [20C] (W.I.; 'ca-ca')

log [1970s+]

●●●●●●●●●●●●●●●●●●●●●●●●●●●●●●●●●●●
Turds large and small

belly flopper [1990s] (a turd that splashes the
buttocks as it enters the water)

chocolate iceberg [1990s] (a turd that is so large
that a part of it is above the water)

chocolate shark [1990s]

dachshund [1990s]

depth charge [1990s]

floater [1990s] (a stool that does not disappear
when the toilet is flushed)

flock of starlings [1990s] (small pieces of
excrement)

Gravesend twins [mid-19C] (solid pieces of
excrement, from the sewerage outfall at
Gravesend)

groaner [1990s]

grogan [1990s] (orig. Aus.)

quaker [18C–19C] (a hard and lengthy piece of
excrement; i.e. it is long, thin, hard and 'wears
brown')

tree log [1990s]

U blocker [1990s] (an exceptionally large stool)

●●●●●●●●●●●●●●●●●●●●●●●●●●●●●●●●●●●

●●●●●●●●●●●●●●●●●●●●●●●●●●●●●●●●●●●
Unusual and surprising turds

airmail [1950s+] (UK prison; parcelled up faeces tossed from a window)

flying pasty [late 18C] (a packet of excrement wrapped in paper and flung over a neighbour's wall)

gypsy's ginger [20C] (a pile of human excrement found out of doors)

kakker-boosah [19C] (prematurely voided excrement)

yen-shee baby [1930s+] (drugs; hard impacted faeces produced, often painfully, by a heroin addict during a period of withdrawal)

●●●●●●●●●●●●●●●●●●●●●●●●●●●●●●●●●●●

lumper [1970s+] (US)

steamer [1950s+]

tantadlin [mid-17C–late 18C]

tantoblin (tart) [mid-17C–late 18C] (a type of large round sweet tart)

toly [1960s+] (?Scot. *toal*, a small round cake)

turd [11C+]

twinkie [1990s]

DINGLEBERRIES

bead curtains [1990s]

clagnut [1990s] (northern dial. *clag*, a sticky mass entangled in hair)

clinkers [1990s] (Aus.)

dags [1950s+] (Aus.)

dangleberries [1990s]

dilberries [mid-19C+]

dingleberries [1930s+]

fart-o-berries [1990s]

gooseberry [1940s]

hairy toffee [1990s]

jubnuts [1990s]

kling-ons [1990s]

mince medallions [1990s]

mustang [1990s]

toffee strings [1990s]

willnots [1990s]

winnet [20C]

SKIDMARKS

blotcher [1970s+] (US campus)

bobstain [1930s+]

Hershey squirts [1980s+] (US campus)

marmite stripe [1990s]

russet gusset [1990s]

skiddies [1930s+]

skidmarks [1930s+]

Tijuana racetrack [1950s+] (US)

ANIMALS' EXCREMENT

barker's egg [1990s] (Aus.; dog excrement)

do [1930s+]

do-do [1930s+]

dog [1960s+]

doggy-do [1960s+]

dog toffee [1990s] (i.e. it readily adheres to the sole of the shoe)

doings [1980s+]

flap [20C]

flop [1950s+] (US)

horse apple/horse biscuit/horse doughnut/horse dumpling [20C] (US; horse excrement)

hot dog [late 19C+]

mallacky [20C] (Irish; cat excrement)

mess [20C]

pooch [1920s+] (dog excrement)

```
o o o o o o o o o o o o o o o o o o o o o o o o o o o o o o o o o
```
Stepping in it ...

cut one's foot [19C+] (US)

cut one's foot with a Dutchman's razor
[19C+] (to step in animal excrement in a field
or farmyard)

```
o o o o o o o o o o o o o o o o o o o o o o o o o o o o o o o o o
```

DIARRHOEA

apple-blossom two-step [20C]

arse-piss [1990s]

back-door trot [late 18C+]

backyard trots [20C]

b.d.t. [20C] ('*back-door trot*')

boot-hill two-step [20C] (US)

bum soup [1990s]

chickenshits [1950s]

chocolate chutney [1990s]

clart [1970s+]

cocktails [1920s+] (Aus.)

collywobbles [mid-19C]

cow's courant [late 18C]

crab-apple two-step [20C] (US; diarrhoea produced by
eating sour fruit)

bum soup

crud [1950s+] (orig. US milit.)

dribbling shits [20C]

drippy tummy [1960s] (US)

drizzlies [1940s–70s] (US)

fantod [19C+] (US)

flying pasty shits [1980s+] (US campus)

green-apple dirties [20C] (US)

green-apple quickstep [1950s+] (US)

green-apple trots [1950s+] (US)

green-apple two-step [1950s+] (US)

green death [1960s–70s] (US campus; sickness and diarrhoea, supposedly caused by student canteen food)

gurry [16C] (Romani *jeer*, excrement)

Hershey squirt [1970s+] (US)

jerry-go-nimble [mid-19C]

johnny trots [20C] (US Appalachian)

movies [20C]

○○○○○○○○○○○○○○○○○○○○○○○○○○○○○○○
Diarrhoea in rhyming slang

Rhyming with 'shits'

Eartha Kitts [1950s+]

Edgar Britts [1960s+]

florins [1990s] (punning on 'two-bob bits')

Jimmy Britts [1940s+]

nicker bits [20C]

threepenny bits [late 19C+]

tomtits [1960s+] (Aus.)

trey-bits [1950s+] (Aus./N.Z.)

two-bob bits [20C]

Zasu Pitts [1930s–50s]

Rhyming with 'trots'

Zachary Scotts [1940s–50s]

○○○○○○○○○○○○○○○○○○○○○○○○○○○○○○○

○○○○○○○○○○○○○○○○○○○○○○○○○○○○○○○○○○○○○○
Ringburners

red ring [1990s] (an inflamed and painful anus
   caused by diarrhoea)

ringburner [1970s+] (UK society; a very painful
   act of defecation)

ring sting [1990s] (an inflamed and painful
   anus caused by diarrhoea)

○○○○○○○○○○○○○○○○○○○○○○○○○○○○○○○○○○○○○○

quick step [mid-19C] (US)

runs [1960s+]

rusty water [1990s]

scatters [19C]

scoot [20C] (Ulster)

scoots [20C] (US campus)

shaster [1990s] (a sudden attack of diarrhoea)

shits [1940s+]

shitters [late 19C+]

skiets [20C] (S. Afr.)

skitters [mid-19C+]

sour-apple quickstep [1990s]

squitters [late 19C+]

trots [early 19C+]

wherry-go-nimble [20C]

TO HAVE DIARRHOEA

blow mud [1990s]

bowel off [20C] (US)

crop spray [1990s]

fly off [20C] (US)

have the pasties [1980s+] (US campus)

piss rusty water [1990s]

pre-pre [1960s] (W.I.)

ride the porcelain bus/ride the porcelain Honda
    [1960s+] (US campus)

run [1960s+]

○○○○○○○○○○○○○○○○○○○○○○○○○○○○○○○○
Suffering from diarrhoea
I could shit through the eye of a needle
    [late 19C+]

in the clarts [1970s+]

loose in the hilt [19C]

loose-legged [19C]

sterky [1930s+] (Aus.: *sterc*oraceous. pertaining
    to faeces)

○○○○○○○○○○○○○○○○○○○○○○○○○○○○○○○○○○

HOLIDAY TUMMIES

Aztec hop [1960s+]

Aztec revenge [1950s+]

Aztec two-step [1950s+]

Bombay belly [1990s+]

Cairo crud [1940s+]

Delhi belly [1940s+]

GIs/GI trots [20C] (US; from the food poisoning to which troops posted abroad are susceptible)

gyppy tummy/gippy tummy [1940s+] (originally contracted in E*gyp*t)

King Tut's revenge [1970s+] (US; diarrhoea contracted in the Middle East)

Mexicali revenge [1970s] (US; from the town of *Mexicali* in Mexico)

Mexican foxtrot [1950s+] (US)

Mexican toothache [1960s+]

Mexican two-step [1950s+]

Montezuma's revenge [1960s+] (orig. US; diarrhoea contracted in Mexico)

Patagonian pasodoble [1990s]

Rangoon runs [1940s+]

Singapore tummy [20C]

wog gut [1950s+]

let a badger loose

TO BREAK WIND

backfire [1950s+]

blitter [20C] (Ulster)

blotch [1970s+]

blow off [20C]

blow one's horn [20C] (US)

break the sound barrier [1960s+] (Can.)

burk [20C] (US)

burn bad powder [1910s–20s]

burst at the broadside [late 17C–mid-19C]

cheese [1950s+]

chuff [1940s+]

crack [20C]

crack a fart [1980s+] (US campus)

cut a finger [late 19C–1900s]

cut the cheese [1950s+]

do one's no-manners [20C] (US)

drop a beast [1970s+] (UK society)

drop a thumper [1960s+]

○○○○○○○○○○○○○○○○○○○○○○○○○○○○○○○○○
To fart in rhyming slang

apple tart [20C] (Aus.)

beef-heart [late 19C]

bullock's heart [late 19C]

D'Oyly Carte [1970s–80s]

gooseberry tart [mid-19C–1930s]

heart and dart [mid-19C–1920s]

horse and cart [1970s]

let go a razzo [1950s+] (i.e. '*ra*spberry tart')

raspberry tart [1950s+]

○○○○○○○○○○○○○○○○○○○○○○○○○○○○○○○○○○

Whoops ...

draw mud from the well [1990s] (to expel a
small amount of faeces when breaking wind)

drop a pebble [1990s] (to pass a small stool while
breaking wind)

follow through [1990s] (to expel a small amount
of faeces when breaking wind)

○○

drop one's guts [1990s]

fart [late 14C+]

float an air biscuit [1990s]

fluff [1960s+] (N.Z. juv./US campus)

foist [late 16C] (to break wind silently)

guff [20C]

gurk [1920s+] (Aus.)

kill the Easter bunny [20C]

let a badger loose [1990s+]

let off [20C]

let one go/let one fly/let one off/let one rip [1970s+]
(US campus)

lose one's manners [20C]

open one's purse [1990s]

poop [early 18C+]

poot [20C] (US)

puff [late 19C+]

pump [1980s+]

quack [1990s+] (to break wind noisily)

shoot the bunny [1980s]

squeak the breeze [1990s]

step on a carpet frog [1990s]

step on a duck [1990s]

strike up the colliery band [1990s]

take an air dump [1990s]

toot [1970s+]

trump [early 15C+]

whistle down the y-fronts [1990s]

THE FART

air biscuit [1990s+]

air buffet [1990s+]

backwards burp [1990s]

bafoon/puffoon [20C] (W.I.)

blanket ripper [1990s]

blurter [1990s+]

bottom burp [1980s+]

breezer [1960s+] (Aus.)

cheeser [early 19C+]

egg McWhiff [1990s+]

fart [late 14C+]

fartick/fartkin [19C]

fizzle [late 18C+] (a gentle or silent fart)

fogo [19C]

grime bubble [1990s]

guff [20C]

hooter [1980s+] (US)

blanket ripper

oooooooooooooooooooooooooooooooooo

S.B.D.s and other pungent farts

Andrex fart [1990s] (from the advertising slogan
  for *Andrex* toilet paper, 'soft, strong and very
  long')

blind fart [late 19C+]

brewer's fart [20C] (a strong-smelling fart)

fice/foyse [late 18C]

foist/foyst [late 16C]

fyst [late 16C]

rim slide [1960s+] (US prison)

room clearer [1990s]

s.b.d. [1960s+] ('*s*ilent *b*ut *d*eadly')

silent but deadly [1990s]

slinky one [late 19C+]

oooooooooooooooooooooooooooooooooo

horse and cart [1970s] (rhy. sl. 'fart')

Jenny Lind [20C] (rhy. sl. 'wind')

one-cheek squeek [1990s]

pocket frog [1990s]

pocket-thunder [19C]

poep [1960s+]

poop [1930s+]

poot [20C]

○○○○○○○○○○○○○○○○○○○○○○○○○○○○○○○○○○○○
Loud farts

barking spiders [1980s+] (US campus)

bomber [1980s+] (US teen)

fat one/fat 'un [19C]

rasper [20C]

rip snorter [mid-19C+] (orig. US)

○○○○○○○○○○○○○○○○○○○○○○○○○○○○○○○○○○○○

pump [late 19C+] (Scot.)

razzler [1990s+]

rectal retort [1990s]

Scotch warming pan/Scots warming-pan [19C]

tail shot [1990s]

thorough cough [late 17C–mid-19C] (a cough accompanied by a simultaneous breaking of wind)

toot [1960s+]

○○○○○○○○○○○○○○○○○○○○○○○○○○○○○○○○○○○○
Wet farts

dirt sauce [1990s]

Hershey squirt [1970s+]

squirt [1980s+]

wet one [late 19C+]

○○○○○○○○○○○○○○○○○○○○○○○○○○○○○○○○○○○○

tree monkey [1990s]

trouser chuff/trouser cough [1980s+]

trump [late 19C–1900s]

trumpet [1990s]

windy pops [20C]

FART TALK

an empty house is better than a bad tenant
  [1930s+]

catch that one and paint it blue [1990s]

do you spit much with that cough? [1910s–20s]
  (Can.)

good evening, vicar [20C]

good health [1990s]

it's the beer talking [1920s+]

more tea, vicar? [20C]

○○○○○○○○○○○○○○○○○○○○○○○○○○○○○○○○○○○○
The ignited fart
afterburner [1990s]

blue dart/blue streak [1990s] (the effect produced by breaking wind next to a lit match)

orange banana [1980s+] (the effect produced by
  breaking wind next to a lit match)

○○○○○○○○○○○○○○○○○○○○○○○○○○○○○○○○○○○○

pin a tail on that [1990s]

sew a button on that [1990s]

there goes the elephant [1990s]

who cut the cheese? [1950s+] (US)

FANNY FARTS

cunt bubble [1990s]

fanny fart [20C]

front bottom burp [1990s]

kweef/queef [1990s]

minge burp [1990s]

○○○○○○○○○○○○○○○○○○○○○○○○○○○○○○○○
Bedroom farts

Dutch oven [1990s] (the smell of a bed in which someone has broken wind)

Greek sauna [1990s] (placing one's partner's head under the duvet after breaking wind)

○○○○○○○○○○○○○○○○○○○○○○○○○○○○○○○○

URINARY
FUNCTIONS

TO URINATE

bleed one's turkey [1920s+]

bleed the liver [1920s+]

do pooley/do poolie [1930s+] (Irish)

do a sip [mid–late 19C] (backslang *sip*, piss)

do one's duty [20C]

give the Chinaman a music lesson [20C] (from the *china* toilet bowl and the *music* it supposedly produces when urinated upon)

have a slash [20C]

have a splash [20C]

kill a snake [19C]

kill a tree [19C]

lag [mid-16C–mid-19C]

lash [1990s] (US)

leak [late 19C+]

make a piss stop [1980s+] (esp. to stop drinking in order to visit the lavatory)

make a puddle [1960s+]

○○○○○○○○○○○○○○○○○○○○○○○○○○○○○○○○○
To urinate in rhyming slang
go for a Leslie [1990s] (i.e. *Leslie Ash*, slash)

Zorba [1950s+] (i.e. *Zorba the Greek*, leak)

○○○○○○○○○○○○○○○○○○○○○○○○○○○○○○○○○○

oooooooooooooooooooooooooooooooooo
Desperate to urinate ...

have one's back teeth afloat [1960s+]

take a Chinese singing lesson [1990s] (to
urinate following a desperate need)

want to piss like a dressmaker [late 19C] (from
dressmakers working in sweatshops who were
not permitted to take a break)

oooooooooooooooooooooooooooooooooo

make pee-pee [1920s+] (usu. juv.)

mingo [late 18C–mid-19C] (US campus)

pay a penny [1950s]

pay one's water bill [1970s] (US Black)

pee [20C]

pee-wee [late 19C+] (juv.)

piddle [late 18C+]

piss [mid-18C+]

piss up a storm [1990s] (US: to urinate for a relatively
long time)

rack off [19C]

run off [19C]

run some water through one's pipe [1970s+]

shed a tear [mid-19C]

shed a tear for Nelson [mid-19C+]

shoot a lion [19C]

sip [1900s] (backslang, 'piss')

slack (off) [late 19C+]

spend a penny [1950s+]

splash one's boots [20C]

take a leak/spring a leak [1910s+] (orig. US)

tiddle [20C]

tinkle [1930s+] (usu. juv.)

waz [1970s+]

wee [1920s+] (mainly juv.)

whiz [1920s+]

widdle [1950s+]

AIMING ARCHIE: THE MALE EXPERIENCE

aim Archie at the Armitage [1960s+]

dangle one's donger [1960s+]

do the gentleman [1920s]

drain one's lizard [20C]

drain the dragon [1960s+]

drain the main vein [1980s+] (US campus)

flog the lizard [1960s+]

go where the big knobs hang out [1960s+]

hang one's meat [1900s–10s] (US)

knock the dew off the lily [1960s+]

leak the lizard [1960s+] (Aus./US)

siphon the python

point percy at the porcelain [1960s+]

shake a sock [20C]

shake the dew off the lily [1960s+]

siphon the python [1960s+] (Aus.)

squeeze the lemon [late 19C+]

wring out one's sock [20C]

wring the dew off the branch [20C]

wring the rattlesnake [20C]

○○○○○○○○○○○○○○○○○○○○○○○○○○○○○○○○

Shaking the lettuce ... (the female experience)

rinse the lettuce [1990s+]

shake the lettuce [1990s+]

○○○○○○○○○○○○○○○○○○○○○○○○○○○○○○○○

WALKING THE DOG

catch a horse [20C] (Aus.)

let one's horse out of the stable [1950s–60s]

lope one's mule [1940s+] (US)

walk one's dog [1960s] (US)

water one's nag [late 17C–mid-18C]

water one's pony [20C]

water the dragon [mid-19C]

water the horses [20C]

water the mule [1990s] (US)

STRAINING AND DRAINING

drain off [19C]

drain one's radiator [1940s+]

pump [mid-19C]

○○○○○○○○○○○○○○○○○○○○○○○○○○○○○○○○○○
Al fresco

burn the grass [20C] (Aus.; to urinate out of doors)

go look at the crops [20C]

look upon a hedge [1930s]

point percy at the pavement [1960s+] (to
urinate on the street)

water the flowers [20C]

○○○○○○○○○○○○○○○○○○○○○○○○○○○○○○○○○○

○○○○○○○○○○○○○○○○○○○○○○○○○○○○○○○○○○○○○
Shaking hands ...

shake hands with an old friend [1960s+]

shake hands with him [1960s+]

shake hands with Mr Right [1960s+]

shake hands with the baby [1960s+]

shake hands with the fellow who stood up when I got married [1960s+]

shake hands with the unemployed [1960s+]

shake hands with the wife's best friend [1960s+]

○○○○○○○○○○○○○○○○○○○○○○○○○○○○○○○○○○○

pump bilge [20C] (US)

pump ship [late 18C+]

strain off [20C]

strain one's greens [1950s+]

strain the potatoes [1960s+] (Aus.)

tap a keg [20C] (US)

tap a kidney [1970s+] (US)

tilt a kidney [1970s+] (US)

URINATION

dip-around [1960s+]

little jobs [20C]

nature's call [20C]

number one [20C]

pee [20C]

pee-pee [1920s+] (usu. juv.)

piddle [late 19C+]

piss [early 19C+]

pisscall [1950s] (a stop for urination during work or on a journey)

pooley/poolie [1930s+] (Irish)

quick one [1910s+]

run-off [1960s]

slash [1930s+]

squirt [1990s]

tinkle [1930s+]

∘∘∘∘∘∘∘∘∘∘∘∘∘∘∘∘∘∘∘∘∘∘∘∘∘∘∘∘∘∘∘
Puddles and dicksplashes

accident [late 19C+] (urination in one's clothing)

dicksplash [1990s] (droplets of urine left on one's underwear after urination)

forget-me-nots [1990s] (droplets of urine left on one's underwear after urination)

puddle [1960s+]

smell like a ram-goat [20C] (W.I.; to smell disgusting, esp. after passing out drunk and urinating down one's legs)

∘∘∘∘∘∘∘∘∘∘∘∘∘∘∘∘∘∘∘∘∘∘∘∘∘∘∘∘∘∘∘∘∘∘∘

ooooooooooooooooooooooooooooooooooooo
Toilet talk

after you with the po, Jane [late 19C–1920s] (a refer-
ence to the need to take turns in using an outdoor
privy; transferred in joc. usage to indoor facilities)

addressed by one male to another on the way to the lavatory:

do one for me [20C]

requiring the response:

which side do you shake it? [20C]

ooooooooooooooooooooooooooooooooooooo

trout fishing [1990s] (*trouser trout* = penis)

waz [1970s+]

wee [1920s+] (mainly juv.)

wet [1920s+]

whiz [1970s]

widdle [1950s+] (mainly juv.)

URINATION IN RHYMING SLANG

Rhyming with 'leak'

bubble and squeak [20C] (Aus.)

Rhyming with 'pee'

Jack Dee [1990s+]

lemon tea [20C]

Peters and Lee [1980s–90s]

riddle-me-ree [20C]

Robert E. (Lee) [20C]

Sammy Lee [20C]

Southend-on-Sea [20C]

Victory V [1940s+]

you and me [20C]

Rhyming with 'piddle' or 'widdle'

dicky diddle [20C]

gerry riddle [1930s+] (Aus.)

hey-diddle-diddle [1950s]

hi-diddle-diddle [1950s]

jerry riddle [mid-19C]

jimmy (riddle) [1930s+]

pig in the middle [20C]

Rhyming with 'piss'

angel's kiss [20C] (Aus.)

apple and pip [late 19C+] (backslang *sip*, piss)

comical chris [1970s–80s]

cousin sis [20C]

cuddle and kiss [1930s+]

goodnight kiss [20C]

gypsy's [20C] (i.e. *gypsy's* kiss)

hit and miss [1960s+]

johnny bliss [20C] (Aus.)

micky bliss/mike bliss [20C]

rattle and hiss [20C]

single fish [1990s]

snake's hiss [20C] (Aus.)

that and this [20C]

Rhyming with 'slash'

Frazer Nash [1970s]

Jackie (Dash) [1960s+]

J. Carroll Naish [1970s]

○○○○○○○○○○○○○○○○○○○○○○○○○○○○○○○○
Sex and slashing

German [20C] (urination on a partner for sexual
stimulation)

golden screw [1960s+] (anal intercourse culmi-
nating in urination rather than ejaculation)

golden shower [1960s+] (urination on a partner
for sexual stimulation)

golden shower queen [1960s+] (a homosexual
who enjoys being urinated on)

water sports [1960s+] (urination on a partner
for sexual stimulation)

w/s [1960s+] (water sports)

○○○○○○○○○○○○○○○○○○○○○○○○○○○○○○○○

Johnny Cash [1960s+]

Pat Cash [1990s]

pie and mash [1970s+]

whiplash [1940s+]

Rhyming with 'tinkle'

Rip van Winkle [20C]

URINE

chamber lye [late 18C–early 19C] (urine standing in a chamberpot)

lag [late 16C–19C]

lemonade [1970s] (US)

number one [20C]

pee [20C]

piddle [late 19C+]

∘∘∘∘∘∘∘∘∘∘∘∘∘∘∘∘∘∘∘∘∘∘∘∘∘∘∘∘∘∘∘∘∘
Two male toilet activities

paisley removal [1990s] (the male habit of trying to remove specks of faeces from the toilet bowl with one's stream of urine)

piss polo [1990s] (the male habit of moving disinfectant tablets in a urinal trough with one's stream of urine)

∘∘∘∘∘∘∘∘∘∘∘∘∘∘∘∘∘∘∘∘∘∘∘∘∘∘∘∘∘∘∘∘∘

water sports

piss [early 19C+]

puddle [1960s+] (a small pool of urine)

salt water [late 17C–early 18C]

scatter [19C]

slash [1930s+]

sweetpea [19C]

tail juice [late 17C–early 18C]

tea [early 18C]

tiddle [20C]

warm beer [1960s+]

wee [1920s+] (mainly juv.)

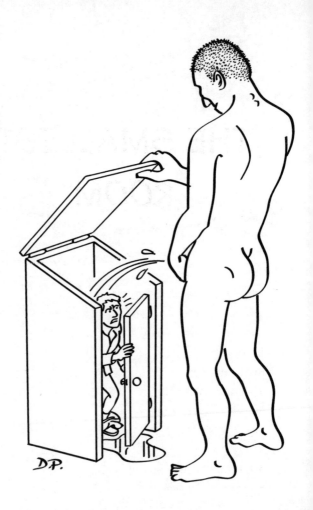

THE SMALLEST ROOM

THE LAVATORY

bog [late 18C+]

cacatorium [19C]

can [19C] (US)

case [late 18C–1900s] (Italian *casa*, a house)

cludgie [1990s] (dial. *cludgy*, sticky, wet and heavy)

compost hole [19C]

crap can [1930s+] (US)

craphouse [1930s+] (orig. US)

crapper [1920s+]

crapping can [1930s+] (US)

dumper [1960s+] (US)

ooooooooooooooooooooooooooooooooo
The loo: five possible etymologies

From French *l'eau* = water

From French *lieux d'aisance* = water closet

From *bordalou*, a portable commode carried by 18C
    ladies in their muffs

From standard English *leeward*, the side of a ship
    turned away from the wind and as such the side
    of over which one would urinate/defecate.

An abbreviation of, or pun on, *Waterloo*, whether
    the station or battle it commemorates

ooooooooooooooooooooooooooooooooo

○○○○○○○○○○○○○○○○○○○○○○○○○○○○○○○○○○○○○
Lavatories of college and campus

forakers [mid-19C] (orig. Winchester College jargon; Latin *forica* or SE *fouracres*, i.e. a field)

fourth [mid-19C] (originally used at Trinity College Cambridge; at that time the college privies were located in the *fourth* court and an undergraduate who had gone there would write on his door 'Gone 4'; an alternative etymology suggests that the undergraduate's morning went through *four* stages: chapel, breakfast, pipe, visit to the lavatory)

growler [1970s+] (US campus; from the noise of someone straining to defecate)

pissoir [1980s+] (US campus)

rear/rears [20C] (orig. US campus; from their position in the *rear* of a college)

○○○○○○○○○○○○○○○○○○○○○○○○○○○○○○○○○○○○○

dunnaken [17C]

dunnyken [18C–19C]

flush [1960s+] (US)

gents [1930s+]

grot [1940s+] (N.Z.)

gutbucket [1940s] (US)

hoohah [1920s+] (the *hoo* of effort followed by the *hah* of relief)

hopper [1970s]

jerry-come-tumble
[mid–late 19C] (*jerry* =
chamberpot or lavatory;
jerry-go-nimble = diar-
rhoea)

lob [20C]

loo [late 19C+]

lulu [late 19C+] (i.e. 'loo')

petty house [19C]

pisshole [1930s+]

pisshouse [20C]

plumbing [1930s–50s]

po [late 19C+] (chamber*pot*)

Quaker's burying ground
[18C–19C] (*quaker* = a
hard and possibly lengthy
piece of excreta)

queer place [1940s–50s]

scent-bottle [late 19C]

Scotch ordinary [late 18C–
early 19C]

scraping castle [mid-19C] (i.e. a place
where one *scrapes* oneself clean)

shithole [19C+]

where the Queen sends nobody

shithouse [17C+]

shit-pit [20C]

shitter [20C] (US)

thunderbox [1930s+] (a portable commode)

**where the Queen goes on foot/where the Queen sends
  nobody** [20C]

wherry-go-nimble [20C]

⚬⚬⚬⚬⚬⚬⚬⚬⚬⚬⚬⚬⚬⚬⚬⚬⚬⚬⚬⚬⚬⚬⚬⚬⚬⚬⚬⚬⚬⚬⚬
Urinals and public lavatories

cottage [late 19C+] (‘*cottage* of convenience’)

dike [1920s+] (Aus.; lit. ‘pit’)

greenhouse [1900s–20s] (Irish; a public toilet)

green man [20C] (a urinal in a public house)

pisser [late 19C+] (a urinal)

pisshole [1930s+] (a urinal)

trap [20C] (a cubicle in a public toilet)

trizzer [1920s+] (Aus.; a public lavatory, from the
    time when the charge for a ‘wash-and-brush-
    up’ was threepence, i.e. a *trizzie*)

used-beer department [1920s+] (Can.; a toilet in
    a bar)

⚬⚬⚬⚬⚬⚬⚬⚬⚬⚬⚬⚬⚬⚬⚬⚬⚬⚬⚬⚬⚬⚬⚬⚬⚬⚬⚬⚬⚬⚬⚬

JAKE, JACK AND JOHN

jakes [early 16C–1900s] (possibly meaning *Jake's* or *Jack's* place, using SE 'Jack' as generic for a man)

jacque's [16C]

jackhouse/jakehouse [16C]

ajax [late 16C] (a pun on 'a jakes')

cuz john/cousin john [mid-18C–mid-19C] (US campus)

jack [late 18C–early 19C]

joe (house) [mid-19C–1930s] (US campus; an outside toilet)

johnny [mid-19C; 1930s+] (US)

john(-house) [1930s+] (orig. US college)

johnny house [1930s+] (US; an outside toilet)

THE LAVATORY IN RHYMING SLANG

Rhyming with 'bog'
Kermit the Frog [1970s]

Rhyming with 'dunny'
don't be funny [20C] (Aus.)

Rhyming with 'piss'
snake's hiss [20C] (Aus.)

Rhyming with 'pisshole'
savoury rissole [20C]

Rhyming with 'shitter'
Tex Ritter [1990s]

oooooooooooooooooooooooooooooooo
Carsey: a word in search of a spelling

carsey [late 19C+] (a privy: Italian *casa*, a house)

carsy [late 19C+]

causey [late 19C+]

cawsey [late 19C+] (a lavatory)

karsey [1960s+]

karsy [1960s+]

karzey [1960s+]

kazi [1960s+]

oooooooooooooooooooooooooooooooo

Rhyming with 'throne'

rag and bone [20C]

Rhyming with 'wash'

lemon and dash [1950s+] (a public toilet)

TOILET EUPHEMISMS 1: PLACES OF BUSINESS

bank [1930s–40s] (US Black)

chamber of commerce [1940s] (US Black)

gingerbread-office [17C] (an outside toilet, from the colour of excrement)

House of Commons [late 18C–mid-19C]

○○○○○○○○○○○○○○○○○○○○○○○○○○○○○○○○○○○○○
The Ladies' lavatory

jane [mid-19C+] (US; playing on 'john')

ladies [1930s+]

ladies' walk [mid-19C]

la vogue [1980s+] (US campus)

○○○○○○○○○○○○○○○○○○○○○○○○○○○○○○○○○○○○○

house of easement [17C] (an outside toilet)

House of Lords [early 19C+]

house of office [17C] (an outside toilet)

library [1930s+] (US; an outside toilet, from the old newspapers left there as lavatory paper)

little office [18C+]

office [early 18C–1960s]

outdoor library [1930s+] (US; an outside toilet)

parliament (house) [late 19C] (an outside toilet)

TOILET EUPHEMISMS 2:
THE COY AND THE CLOYING

altar [20C]

aunt [mid-19C–1920s+] (UK society)

auntie [mid-19C+]

closet of ease [late 17C]

double-U [late 19C–1910s] (i.e. 'W')

geography [1920s+]

little boy's room [1930s+] (orig. US)

little girl's room [1940s+] (orig. US)

my aunt's [early 19C–1900s]

necessaries [17C]

om-tiddly-om-pom [1910s–30s]

place [1900s–50s]

place of convenience/place of resort [17C]

place where one coughs [1920s+]

smallest room [1930s+]

temple [20C]

throne [1920s+]

W [1950s+] (W.C.)

you know where [20C]

throne

DUBS AND DUNNIES: THE ANTIPODEAN LAVATORY

brassco [1960s+] (Aus.: 'where the *brass* knobs *go*')

diddy [1950s+] (Aus. juv.)

dub [1940s+] (Aus./N.Z.)

dunnigan [20C] (Aus.)

dunny [1930s+] (Aus.)

leakhouse [1940s+] (Aus.)

shouse [1940s+] (Aus.; *shithouse*)

snake's house [20C] (orig. Aus.; *snake's hiss* = piss)

toot [1960s+] (Aus.)

van dyke [1920s+] (Aus.; playing on *dike*)

THE OUTSIDE LAVATORY

apple-knocker [20C] (US; it is situated beneath an *apple* tree and the user can hear apples *knocking* on its roof)

back [mid-19C+] (US)

backhouse [late 19C+]

backy [late 19C+] (US)

backyard telephone booth [20C] (US)

biffy [1930s+] (US; military jargon, 'small shelter')

boggard [16C]

boghouse [late 17C+]

bog-shop [mid-19C–1900s]

California house [20C] (US)

chapel of ease [17C–mid-19C]

chicken coop [20C] (US)

chic sale [1940s+] (US; *Chic Sale* was a builder of privies)

coffee-house [late 18C] (from the colour of faeces)

coffee-shop [late 18C–mid-19C]

colfabias [mid-19C] (fake Latin)

college [19C] (US)

commons [late 18C–mid-19C]

convenience [19C]

crapping casa [mid-19C]

crapping case [mid-19C]

crapping castle [mid-19C]

crapping ken/cropping ken [late 18C–mid-19C]

○○○○○○○○○○○○○○○○○○○○○○○○○○○○○○○○○○○○○
Mrs Jones's house

casey jones [1960s+] (playing on Mrs *Jones*'s house + *carsey*)

Mrs Jones [mid-19C]

Mrs Jones's house [mid-19C]

Mrs Murphy [1960s+]

Mother Jones [1930s+] (US; an outdoor privy, from the US labour leader Mary Harris, 1837–1930, also known as *Mother Jones*)

neighbour jones [1930s–40s] (US; an outdoor privy)

Widow Jones [mid-19C]

Widow Jones's house [mid-19C]

○○○○○○○○○○○○○○○○○○○○○○○○○○○○○○○○○○○○○

○○○○○○○○○○○○○○○○○○○○○○○○○○○○○○○○○○○○○○○
Privies of the Great Depression

F.D.R./F.D. Roosevelt [1930s–40s] (US; under President *F.D. Roosevelt*, 1933–45, new outdoor toilets were built in deprived rural areas as part of the New Deal)

Federal building [20C] (US; an outside toilet)

first national bank [20C] (US; an outside toilet, from the resentment of farmers towards the banks, which regularly repossessed their land when times got hard)

hoover [1930s] (US; the administration of US President Herbert *Hoover*, 1929–33, saw the worst years of the Depression)

○○○○○○○○○○○○○○○○○○○○○○○○○○○○○○○○○○○○○○○

danna [late 18C–mid-19C]

dollar house [20C] (US)

doll house [20C]

donagher [early 19C–1920s]

dumpty [1960s+] (Aus./N.Z.)

dumpty-doo [1960s+] (Aus./N.Z.)

dumpy [1960s+] (Aus./N.Z.)

dunny [1930s+] (Aus.)

Egypt [19C+] (US; i.e. a far distant place)

flaming fury [1960s] (Aus.; from the periodic burning off of its contents)

garden house [20C] (US)

head [19C] (from nautical jargon for a ship's lavatory, originally sited at the *head* of the ship, near the bowsprit)

honey house [20C] (US; *honey* = excrement)

hoosegow [20C] (US; Spanish *juzgado*, a court of justice)

ivy cottage [late 19C+]

jericho [mid-18C–late 19C]

Kalahari wishing well [1970s+] (S. Afr.)

kleinhuisie [1960s+] (S. Afr.; Afrikaans, 'little house')

kybo/kibo [1960s–70s] (US; rhy. sl. *khyber pass*, arse)

little barn [20C] (US)

little house [late 19C+] (Aus./N.Z./US)

long drop [1970s+] (S. Afr.)

maggie and jiggs [1950s–60s] (US)

my uncle's [late 18C–early 19C]

necessary [early 17C–mid-19C]

one-holer [20C] (an outside toilet with one seat only)

piccaninny kaya/piccaninny kia/p.k. [1960s+] (S. Afr.; lit. 'Black person's house')

Sears Roebuck library [20C] (US; from the popular use of the old *Sears Roebuck* catalogues as lavatory paper)

shit jacket [1970s] (US Black)

A cottager's A–Z

abdicated [1960s+] (gay; ordered out of the public lavatory where one is looking for sex)

black-'n'-deckering [1990s] (drilling a hole between cubicles in a public lavatory in order to spy on one's neighbour)

bosching [1990s] (drilling a hole between cubicles in a public lavatory in order to spy on one's neighbour)

cottage crawl [1950s+] (gay; to frequent public lavatories for sex)

crapper dick [20C] (US; a policeman who hangs around public lavatories in the hope of entrapping gay men having sex)

dethroned [1950s–60s] (gay; ordered out of the public lavatory where one is looking for sex)

have a cup of tea [1960s+] (to have sex in a public lavatory)

make a milk run [1990s] (US gay; to hang around a men's lavatory looking for sex)

sports bag [1990s] (a bag in which one partner stands in order to avoid his feet being seen by the lavatory attendant while having sex in a cubicle)

●●●●●●●●●●●●●●●●●●●●●●●●●●●●●●●●●●●●

siege [15C]

smokeshell [19C] (from the vapour that rises from hot urine in cold weather)

spice island [early–mid-19C]

stool of ease [17C]

THE COTTAGE: THE PUBLIC CONVENIENCE AS A SEXUAL VENUE

bif [1950s–70s] (US)

cafeteria [1980s+] (US gay; i.e. a place where one goes to 'eat')

clubhouse [1950s–70s] (US)

cottage [1950s+] (gay)

fairy's phonebooth [1960s+] (US gay)

greenhouse [1950s–70s] (US)

lollipop stop [1980s+] (US gay)

lonelyhearts' club [1950s–70s] (US)

luncheonette [1950s–70s] (US)

marble palace [1950s–70s] (US)

penile colony [1950s–70s] (US; punning on *penal colony*)

service station [1980s+] (US gay)

tearoom [1950s+] (US gay)

trading post [1950s–70s] (US)

zipper club [1980s+] (US gay)

ooooooooooooooooooooooooooooooooooo
On the toilet
enthroned [1950s–60s]

on the pot [early 19C+]

ooooooooooooooooooooooooooooooooooo

TO VISIT THE LAVATORY

be excused [1950s+] (mainly school)

chase a rabbit [20C] (US)

do one's business [mid-19C+]

give one's bum an airing [1940s–50s]

go and see uncle [1900s–10s]

go round the corner [late 19C+]

go somewhere [1920s+]

make a pit stop [1980s+]

pay a call [1950s+]

pick the daisies [19C]

pluck a rose [17C+]

see a man about a dog [mid-19C+]

see Mrs Murray [late 19C+]

see one's aunt/see the aunt/see auntie [mid-19C–1920s+]
    (UK society)

take a trip to the bank [1930s–40s] (US Black)

turn the car around [1990s+]

visit Miss Murphy [20C]

visit Mrs Chant's [1920s]

visit Mrs Jones [mid-19C]

visit Mrs Jones's house [mid-19C]

visit my aunt [mid-19C]

visit Sir Harry [mid-19C]

visit the sandbox [20C]

LAVATORY PAPER

Alabama kleenex [1960s+] (US)

ammunition [19C+]

arse-paper [1930s+] (N.Z.)

arsewipe [1950s+]

ass gasket [1990s] (US campus; the paper protector that is placed over a lavatory seat to indicate its sanitized state)

ass paper [1930s+] (US)

ass-wipe [1950s+]

batty paper [20C] (W.I.)

bog bumf [20C]

bogroll [20C]

bumf [late 19C+] ('*bum-*fodder')

bum-fodder [late 17C+]

bum wad [20C] (US)

bungwad [1920s] (US)

burly [20C]

IN CASE OF FIRE
BREAK GLASS

Arkansas fire extinguisher

bushman's friend [1970s+] (N.Z.: any large-leaved plant
that can be used as lavatory paper)

buttwipe [1970s+] (US)

curl paper [late 19C] (*curl* = a piece of excrement)

film for your brownie [1990s+] (punning on the *Brownie*
camera)

fodder [late 19C+]

tail timber [late 19C]

torch-cul [late 17C–18C] (French, 'give one's arse a
  quick smack')

wipe [1950s+]

PISSPOTS AND THUNDERMUGS: THE CHAMBER POT

Arkansas fire extinguisher [20C] (US)

article [early 19C]

badger [19C] (US)

bishop [19C–1900s]

chimmy [1950s+] (W.I.)

convenience [19C]

guzunder [20C] (it 'goes under' the bed)

it [20C]

jereboam [mid-19C]

jerker [late 19C]

jockum gage [17C–18C] (lit. 'penis pot')

jordain/jordan/jurden [early 15C–mid-18C]

lagging gage [18C–19C] (lit. 'urine pot')

left-handed sugar bowl [1950s+] (US)

looking glass [early 17C–mid-19C] (from one's reflection
  in the urine, as well, possibly, as the attention paid by
  contemporary physicians to the urine itself)

mastercan [19C]

member mug [late 17C–early 19C]

mingo [late 18C–mid-19C] (US campus; Latin *mingere*, to urinate)

mug [mid-19C–1950s] (US)

night glass [1940s] (W.I.)

oooooooooooooooooooooooooooooooo
Jemima and Jerry: some 'named' chamber pots

betty [mid-19C] (a generic servant's name)

charlie [20C]

charlie whitehouse [20C] (US; from the *white*ness of the pot)

jemima [late 19C–1900s] (a generic servant's name)

jerry [mid-19C+]

Sir John [early 19C]

twiss [18C] (Irish; an attack on the English writer Richard *Twiss* who had published the highly critical 'Tour in Ireland'. To take their revenge the Irish produced a chamberpot with a picture of Richard Twiss inside it, beneath which was inscribed the rhyme 'Let everyone piss/On lying Dick Twiss')

oooooooooooooooooooooooooooooooo

number one [20C]

Oliver's skull [late 17C–late 19C] (from the Restoration's hatred of *Oliver* Cromwell)

pisspot [mid-18C+]

posie [20C] (W.I.)

pottie [19C+]

potty [19C+]

remedy critch [late 18C–early 19C] (*critch* = earthenware pot)

rogue with one ear [late 17C–early 18C]

smokehouse [19C] (from the vapour that rises from hot urine in cold weather)

smoker [19C]

tea voider [late 18C–late 19C]

thundermug [1930s+]

∘∘∘∘∘∘∘∘∘∘∘∘∘∘∘∘∘∘∘∘∘∘∘∘∘∘∘∘∘∘∘∘∘∘∘∘∘∘
Fun with chamberpots

christen [late 19C+] (to shower someone with the contents of a chamberpot)

crown [20C] (Aus. student: to shower someone with the contents of a chamberpot)

∘∘∘∘∘∘∘∘∘∘∘∘∘∘∘∘∘∘∘∘∘∘∘∘∘∘∘∘∘∘∘∘∘∘∘∘∘∘

SEXUAL
FUNCTIONS: MALE

TO EJACULATE

bang off [1990s+]

blob off [1990s+]

blurt [1990s+]

bust [late 19C+] (US Black)

bust a shot [1950s+] (US Black)

cheese [1950s+]

chuck one's load [1990s]

chunk [1980s+] (US)

come one's cocoa [1970s+]

come one's fat/come one's lot [1970s+]

cough one's yoghurt [1990s+]

crack one's marbles [1930s] (US)

crack one's nuts [1940s–60s] (US)

cream [1950s+]

do it [18C+]

fall in the furrow [20C]

fetch [late 19C+]

fire [late 19C+] (Aus./US)

fire a shot [late 19C+]

get one's balls off [1960s+] (orig. US)

get one's cookies off [1950s+]

get one's gun (off) [1950s+]

get one's jones off [1960s+] (orig. US Black)

●●●●●●●●●●●●●●●●●●●●●●●●●●●●●●●●●●
To ejaculate skilfully

double one's milt [19C] (to ejaculate twice
without withdrawing)

follow through [20C] (to ejaculate twice without
withdrawal)

have a double shot [20C] (to ejaculate twice
during the same session of love-making)

spray someone's tonsils [1930s+] (gay: to
ejaculate in one's partner's mouth)

whitewash someone's tonsils [1960s+] (US: to
ejaculate in one's partner's mouth)

●●●●●●●●●●●●●●●●●●●●●●●●●●●●●●●●●

●●●●●●●●●●●●●●●●●●●●●●●●●●●●●●●●●
The virtuoso ejaculation

double-barrel [1990s] (for a man, more than one
orgasm in one session of sex)

face-painting [1980s+] (ejaculation on one's
partner's face)

facial [1970s+] (ejaculation on one's partner's
face)

grand finale [1990s] (ejaculation on one's
partner's face)

●●●●●●●●●●●●●●●●●●●●●●●●●●●●●●●●●

○○○○○○○○○○○○○○○○○○○○○○○○○○○○○○○○
To ejaculate ineptly – or not at all

fire a blank [1950s+] (to have an orgasm without ejaculation)

fire in the air [19C] [late 19C+] (to ejaculate outside one's partner's body)

have a full bag on [1990s] (to have gone without ejaculation for a long period)

shampoo the rug [1990s] (to ejaculate onto a pubic mound)

shoot one's bolt [20C] (to ejaculate prematurely)

shoot over the stubble [18C–19C] (to ejaculate prematurely)

○○○○○○○○○○○○○○○○○○○○○○○○○○○○○○○○

get one's nuts off [1930s+] (orig. US Black)

give one's gravy [19C]

jam off [1990s+]

jet one's juice [late 19C–1900s]

jiz [late 19C+]

jollop [1990s]

lose one's mess [1990s+]

pop one's nuts [1920s+] (orig. US)

ranch [1990s]

ready to spit [20C] (on the verge of orgasm)

send out the troops [1990s]

skeet [20C] (US Black)

slime [20C] (Aus.)

spaff [1990s+]

spend [mid-17C–late 19C]

spew [20C] (US campus)

splooge [1980s+] (US campus)

spoo [1980s+] (US campus)

spooch [1980s+] (US campus)

spoof [1910s+] (Aus.)

spreck up [1990s+]

spunk (off) [late 19C+] (orig. US)

spurt one's curd [1990s]

squirt one's juice [20C]

tip one's concrete [1990s+]

tip one's dirt [20C]

unload [1960s+]

unload the baby gravy [1990s]

∘∘∘∘∘∘∘∘∘∘∘∘∘∘∘∘∘∘∘∘∘∘∘∘∘∘∘∘∘∘∘∘∘
Rhyming ejaculations
chuck one's muck [1990s]

spew one's goo [1990s]

splatter one's batter [1990s]

∘∘∘∘∘∘∘∘∘∘∘∘∘∘∘∘∘∘∘∘∘∘∘∘∘∘∘∘∘∘∘∘∘

The incompetent ejaculation

dry bob [late 17C+] (sex without ejaculation)

dry fuck [1930s+] (an unsatisfactory act of intercourse, esp. one that does not result in ejaculation or orgasm)

flash in the pan [1980s+] (sex without ejaculation)

loaded gun [1980s+] (the penis before ejaculation of its *load* of semen)

lover's nuts [1940s+] (aches in the testicles caused by sexual stimulation without ejaculation)

○○

BLOWING

blow one's cork [1930s+]

blow one's dust [1960s–70s]

blow one's hump [1950s+] (US)

blow one's juice [1990s]

blow one's load [1990s]

blow one's lot [1940s+] (Aus.)

blow one's lump [late 19C–1920s] (US)

blow one's muck [1990s+]

blow one's tubes [1990s]

blow one's wad [1990s+] (US)

SHOOTING

blow one's cork

shoot [late 19C+]

shoot off [1960s+]

shoot one's load [1920s+]

shoot one's milt [mid-19C–1910s]

shoot one's rocks [1940s+]

shoot one's roe [mid-19C–1900s]

shoot one's wad [1920s+] (orig. US)

shoot white [late 19C]

ORGASMS

big O [1950s+]

blast-off [1960s] (US)

bust [1960s] (US Black)

cock [1960s+] (US Black)

come [mid-17C+]

cum [1920s+]

double master-blaster [1980s] (an orgasm reached through fellatio and the simultaneous smoking of a pipe of crack cocaine)

final gallop [1990s]

flock of sparrows flying out of one's backside [1950s+] (Aus.: the sensation of the male orgasm)

jolly [1960s+] (US)

load [1920s+] (US)

nut [1960s+] (US)

paradise strokes [20C] (the last thrusts that immediately precede orgasm)

pop [mid-19C+]

short strokes [20C] (the last thrusts that immediately precede orgasm)

thrill [1910s+]

TO ACHIEVE ORGASM

blast off [1960s] (US)

blow [1970s+] (orig. US)

bust a nut [1990s]

bust one's kicks off [1920s+] (US)

come [mid-17C+]

come off [17C+]

cum [1950s+]

get a nut [1990s]

get off [1970s+] (orig. US Black)

get off the button [1930s] (US)

get one's kicks off [1920s+] (US)

get one's rocks off [1940s+]

get there [mid-19C+]

go [18C]

go off [1920s+]

go up the rainbow [1970s]

kick the beam [1900s–20s]

let go [late 19C+]

light off [late 19C+]

light up [1940s–50s]

make it [1950s+] (US)

melt [mid-19C+]

plug in the neon [1960s+] (US gay: to inhale amyl nitrate at the moment of orgasm)

make the chimney smoke

pop (off) [1940s+]

pop one's cork [1960s+]

pop one's drawers [1970s]

TO GIVE A WOMAN AN ORGASM

bring on the china [1900s–30s]

bring her off [20C]

bust her out [1980s+] (US Black)

do her job for her [mid-19C+]

get her home [19C]

give her a thrill [1910s+]

make her love come down [1950s–60s] (US Black)

make the chimney smoke [mid-19C+]

pop her cookies [1970s+]

pop her nuts [1950s+]

pop her off [1950s+] (orig. US)

ring her bell [1910s+]

ring her chimes [1970s+] (orig. US)

TO MAKE SOMEONE PREGNANT

big [1950s] (US/W.I.)

blow up [early 17C–1930s] (US)

do a job [20C] (Aus.)

fill in [1950s+] (Aus.)

give a belly [20C] (W.I.)

jag [late 19C]

knock up [mid-18C–19C] (orig. US)

sew up [19C–1940s]

spoil a woman's shape [late 17C–late 19C]

start something [1940s+]

stork [1970s] (US campus)

tie up [19C+]

SEMEN

ammunition [18C]

axle grease [20C]

bip [1990s] (Can.)

bullet [1960s] (US)

chism [late 19C+] (orig. US)

cock puke [1990s]

cock snot [1990s]

come [1920s+]

comings [mid-19C+]

crud/krud [1950s+]

cum [1920s+]

cundy [1990s] (the post-coital mix of semen and vaginal secretions: *cunt* + *dick*)

Semen in rhyming slang

Rhyming with 'spunk'

Harry Monk [20C]

Maria Monk [late 19C+]

pineapple chunk [1990s] (Scots)

Thelonius Monk [20C]

Victoria Monk [late 19C–1900s]

Rhyming with 'cum'

Pedigree Chum [20C]

○○

dicksplash [1990s]

dog water [1960s+] (US)

face cream [1980s+] (US gay)

fetch [19C] (i.e. that which is *fetched* or drawn forth)

gak [20C]

gism/gissum/gizm/gizzum/gyzm [late 19C+] (orig. US)

gloy [20C] (the brandname of a type of 'glue')

glue [late 19C]

goo(-goo) [20C] (orig. US)

herbalz [1990s] (US Black)

jazz [1930s] (US)

jism/jism/jizzum/jiz/jizz [late 19C+] (orig. US)

jit [1970s] (US campus; *jet*)

jollop [1990s+]

joombye [1990s]

knob snot [1990s]

lather [19C–1900s]

○○○○○○○○○○○○○○○○○○○○○○○○○○○○○○○○○○○
Seminal specialities

Irish confetti [20C] (gay; extravagantly ejaculated semen)

jelly jewellery [1990s+] (ejaculated semen covering the face and throat of one's partner)

pearl necklace [1990s] (drops of semen ejaculated onto a partner's neck after fellatio)

snowball [1990s] (semen that has been ejaculated in one's partner's mouth and then returned via a kiss)

soggy biscuit [1960s] (orig. Aus.; a masturbation game, popular among schoolboys, whereby the participants masturbate and then ejaculate onto a biscuit; the last to reach orgasm must eat the semen-covered biscuit)

Uncle Albert's beard [1990s+] (semen that has been ejaculated over the partner's face and throat)

○○○○○○○○○○○○○○○○○○○○○○○○○○○○○○○○○○○

letchwater [19C]

load [1920s+] (US)

lump [late 19C–1920s] (US)

mess [1990s]

mettle [late 18C–early 19C]

milt [19C] (lit. 'roe')

muck [1990s]

ointment [late 18C–late 19C]

paste [1980s+]

pearl [1980s+] (US gay)

pearly passion potion [1990s]

pecker snot [1990s] (US)

population paste [1980s+]

scum [1960s+] (US)

slime [19C+]

snot [1980s+]

spence [20C] (W.I.: lit. 'spendings')

spend [late 19C]

spendings [mid–late 19C]

spew [1980s+] (US campus)

splooge [1980s+] (US campus)

spoo [1980s+] (US campus)

spooch [1980s+] (US campus)

spoof [1910s+] (Aus.)

spooge [1990s] (US)

spratz [1980s+] (US)

spudwater [1990s]

spuff [1990s]

spume [1990s]

spunk [late 19C+]

squirt [1980s+]

tallow [19C]

wad [20C]

white swallow [1990s] (US, mainly West Coast)

COMESTIBLE

baby gravy [1990s]

batter [1990s]

beef gravy [1980s+] (US gay)

cocoa [1970s+]

come-juice [20C]

cream [late 19C+]

creamed beef [1990s]

dick drink [1980s+] (US gay)

duck butter [1930s+] (US)

French dressing [1950s+] (US gay)

French-fried ice-cream [1950s+]

gnat butter [1900s–40s] (US)

gravy [mid-18C+]

honey [19C+]
hot fat [1990s]
jam [1960s+] (US Black)
jelly [17C–19C]
joy juice [1980s+] (US)
juice [early 18C+]

French dressing

living sauce [1990s]

love juice [late 19C+]

manfat [1990s]

nut [1990s] (US)

oyster [late 17C+]

pudding [late 17C+]

roe [mid-19C–1900s]

soul sauce [1980s+] (US gay)

Spanish rice [1960s]

sugar [1920s+] (US Black)

water of life [1950s+] (US Black)

●●●●●●●●●●●●●●●●●●●●●●●●●●●●●●●●●●
Love custard and other dairy products

bollock yoghurt [1990s]

butter [late 19C+]

creamy love bullets [1990s]

custard [1950s] (Aus.)

hot milk [19C]

love custard [1990s]

man's milk [1990s]

melted butter [19C]

milk [mid-17C+]

whipped cream [1970s+] (US Black)

●●●●●●●●●●●●●●●●●●●●●●●●●●●●●●●●●●

SMEGMA

cheese [mid-19C+] (US)

cheesy head [1990s] (a penis that has not been cleansed of smegma)

cock cheese [mid-19C+]

corn on the cob [1990s]

crunt [1950s–60s] (US Black)

dick dolcelatte [1980s]

duck butter [1930s+] (US)

flute feta [1990s]

fumunda cheese [1980s+] (US campus)

gnat butter [1900s-40s] (US)

headcheese [20C]

helmet halva [1980s]

helmet havarti [1980s]

knob cheese [mid-19C+]

John-Thomas Jarlsberg [1980s]

monterey jack [1990s] (US)

nob stilton [1990s]

pecker cheese [1990s]

pecker pecorino [1990s]

todger tilsit [1980s]

willy wensleydale [1980s]

SEXUAL
FUNCTIONS:
FEMALE

MENSTRUATION

THE PERIOD

baker flying [20C] (*baker* = B; in nautical jargon the flag
signifying the second letter of the alphabet is red)

beno [1950s+] (i.e. there will *be no* sex)

big X [1980s+] (US campus)

blitz [20C] (US)

blood and sand [20C] (usu. male use)

bloody monthlies [20C]

collywobbles [mid-19C] (US)

come around [20C] (US)

○○○○○○○○○○○○○○○○○○○○○○○○○○○○○○○○○○○
Friends and relations

Aunt Flo [1950s+] (US; punning on 'flow')

Aunt Jody [20C] (US)

country cousin [19C+] (US)

grandma (George) [late 19C+] (US)

granny [1920s+] (US)

granny grunt/granny chills [20C] (US)

friend [20C] (US Black)

little friend [1920s+] (orig. Can./Aus.)

my friend [20C] (Aus./Ulster/US)

○○○○○○○○○○○○○○○○○○○○○○○○○○○○○○○○○○○

communists [1930s] (US)

curse (of God) [20C]

domestic afflictions [mid–late 19C]

flagging [1930s] (US)

flowers [late 18C–late 19C]

joey [20C]

john [1950s] (US)

monthlies [late 19C+]

monthly bill/monthly dues [20C] (US)

mother nature [20C] (US)

red mary [20C] (US Black)

roses [mid-19C–1920s]

tommy [late 19C+]

visitor [1940s+]

●○●○●○●○●○●○●○●○●○●○●○●○●○●○●○
Dog-days and rag weeks

dog-days [1950s] (US)

period drama [1990s] (the time of a woman's period when she is traditionally moody and short-tempered)

poorly time [late 19C]

rag week [1980s+]

wallflower week [20C] (the duration of a woman's period during which traditionally she is sexually inactive)

●○●○●○●○●○●○●○●○●○●○●○●○●○●○●○

period drama

TO MENSTRUATE

come around [20C] (US)

come crook [1950s] (Aus.)

come on [20C] (to start menstruation)

come sick [20C] (US)

cover the waterfront [20C] (US)

entertain the general [20C] (US)

fall off the roof [1960s+]

flood [1920s–30s] (US Black)

have a friend/have friends to stay [20C] (US Black)

have a little visitor [1920s+]

have the buns on [20C] (Aus.)

have the decorators in/have the painters in [mid-19C+]

have the monkies [1950s–60s] (US)

ride a cotton horse [20C]

ride a white horse [20C]

stub one's toe [20C]

surf the crimson wave [1980s+] (US teen)

○○○○○○○○○○○○○○○○○○○○○○○○○○○○○○○○○○○○○○
Flying the flag
flash the red rag [early 19C–1900s]

fly the flag [mid-19C]

fly the red flag [20C]

have red sails in the sunset [20C]

have the flag out [20C]

have the rag on [1950s+]

put one's flags out [20C]

ride the rag [1940s+]

○○○○○○○○○○○○○○○○○○○○○○○○○○○○○○○○○○○○○○

MENSTRUATING

all white and spiteful [20C]

at number one London [19C]

back in the saddle (again) [1950s+] (US)

caught a rat [1990s]

danger signal is up [late 19C+] (US)

flag is up [late 19C+] (US)

flying baker [20C]

gal's at the stockyards [20C] (US)

gator bit [20C] (US)

monkey is sick [1950s–60s]

monkey has got a haemorrhage [1950s–60s]

on the blob [1990s] (US)

on the rag [1930s+]

o.t.r. [1960s+] (US campus; *on the rag*)

road making [mid–late 19C]

○○○○○○○○○○○○○○○○○○○○○○○○○○○○○○
The menstruating woman

bloody mary [1960s+] (US)

p.m.s. monster [1980s+] (US campus; abbr.
pre-menstrual syndrome)

ribena [1990s]

red dog on a white horse [1970s+] (US Black)

○○○○○○○○○○○○○○○○○○○○○○○○○○○○○○

road up for repairs [mid–late 19C]

so [mid-19C+]

so-so [mid–late 19C]

squiffy [1930s+] (teen)

THE ENCRYPTED PERIOD

Aunt Flo is visiting [20C]

auntie coming to town [20C] (W.I.)

Aunt Jody's come with her suitcase [20C]

Aunt Minnie is visiting [20C]

captain is at home [late 18C–mid-19C]

cardinal is come [late 18C–mid-19C]

george called [20C] (Aus./US)

grandma's coming [late 19C+] (US)

granny's coming [20C] (Aus./US)

Kit has come [late 19C+]

looks like a wet weekend [20C] (orig. Aus.)

Mickey Mouse is kaput [1930s–40s] (US; sex is impossible
    because of menstruation)

my little friend has come [1920s+] (orig. Can./Aus.)

my redheaded aunt has arrived [20C]

Red Sea is out [20C]

see anything? [mid-19C] (asked by a man of a woman and
    meaning, 'have you had your period?')

there's a letter in the post office [mid-19C+] (US)

○○
The overdue period

late [1960s+] (of a woman, whose menstrual
period has failed to occur at the expected time)

miss the boat [1960s] (to miss a menstrual
period)

overdue [1960s+] (of a woman, not having had a
menstrual period at the expected time)

○○

SEX DURING MENSTRUATION

blood sports [1990s] (cunnilingus on a menstruating woman)

cherry blossom kiss [1990s] (oral sex with a woman during
her menstrual period)

jam supper [1990s] (cunnilingus on a menstruating woman)

Mexican lipstick [1990s+] (smears of blood around the
mouth of one who has been having cunnilingus with a
menstruating woman)

pasata grin [1990s+] (smears of blood around the mouth of
one who has been having cunnilingus with a menstruating
woman)

rainbow kiss [1990s] (US: a passionate kiss, which follows an
orgasm reached through reciprocal oral sex between a man
and a menstruating woman, and thus involves the mixing of
semen, vaginal secretions and blood in the mouth)

Mexican lipstick

rainbow necker [1990s] (a person who has oral sex with a
    women while she is menstruating)

red wings [1950s+] (cunnilingus with a menstruating
    woman)

salsa dip [1990s]

○○○○○○○○○○○○○○○○○○○○○○○○○○○○○○○○○○
Multiple orgasms
come a river [mid-17C+]

toot one's train [1970s+]

○○○○○○○○○○○○○○○○○○○○○○○○○○○○○○○○○○

The pink and the brown

if they're old enough to bleed, they're old enough to butcher [1960s+] (if a girl is old enough to menstruate she is old enough for intercourse)

when the red is over the pink, go for the brown [1990s] (when a woman is menstruating, opt for anal intercourse)

when the road runs red, hit the dirt track [1990s] (when a woman is menstruating, opt for anal intercourse)

ooooooooooooooooooooooooooooooooo

VAGINAL SECRETIONS

bitch butter [1970s]

clamjam [1990s]

come [mid-17C+]

cooze [1920s+] (US)

cream [late 19C+]

crotch cheese [1960s+] (unwashed vaginal secretions)

crotch oil [1980s+]

drippings [18C]

fanny batter [1990s]

flap snot [1990s]

French dip [1950s+]

fud slush [1990s+]

goose-grease [late 19C]

gravy [mid-18C+]

grease [1960s+] (US Black)

jelly baby [1920s+] (*jelly* = vagina)

juice [late 17C+]

love juice [late 19C+]

piss [mid-18C+] (to issue vaginal secretions)

snail trail [1990s+] (vaginal secretions marking the underwear)

PREGNANCY

PREGNANT

apron-up [19C+]

away the trip [20C] (Scot.)

awkward [late 19C–1910s]

belly-up [17C–1900s]

bigged [1950s] (US Black)

caught (out) [mid-19C+]

clubbed [1970s+]

clucky [1940s+] (Aus./N.Z.)

coming [late 17C–19C]

cut in the back [mid-17C–mid-19C]

cut in the leg [late 17C–late 18C]

double-ribbed [19C]

embarrassed [1960s] (W.I.)

fallen on [1930s+]

fat [1950s+] (US Black)

full in the belly [late 19C]

full of it [late 19C]

full up [20C] (W.I.)

get a belly [20C] (W.I.)

gone [mid-19C+]

gone overboard [20C] (W.I./St Kitts)

high-bellied/high in the belly [mid–late 19C] (in the last stages of pregnancy)

hit on the master vein [16C]

how-come-ye-so [mid-19C; 20C]

in a fix [20C] (US)

in for it [1910s–20s]

○○○○○○○○○○○○○○○○○○○○○○○○○○○○○○○○○○
Two pregnant tummies
bay window [mid–late 19C]

bellyful of marrow-pudding [mid-19C]

○○○○○○○○○○○○○○○○○○○○○○○○○○○○○○○○○○

○○○○○○○○○○○○○○○○○○○○○○○○○○○○○○○○○○○○○
Pregnancy itself

Egyptian flu [1960s] (US; i.e. one is going to be a
  'mummy')

interesting condition/interesting situation [early
  19C+]

Irish toothache [19C]

i.t.a. [19C] ('Irish toothache')

Paddy's toothache [19C]

pudding club [20C]

○○○○○○○○○○○○○○○○○○○○○○○○○○○○○○○○○○○○○

in pig [1940s+]

in pod [late 19C+]

in the club [20C]

in the familiar way [late 19C]

in the family way [18C+]

in the flue [19C]

in the pudding club [1930s+]

in the spud line [1930s+]

in the straw [mid-19C+] (in labour)

in trouble [late 19C+] (pregnant and unmarried)

jacked up [1900s–10s] (US)

kidded [late 19C–1900s]

knapped [early–mid-19C] (UK Und.; lit. 'taken')

knocked up [mid-19C+] (orig. US)

like that [1970s+] (US, mainly South)

loaded [late 19C+] (orig. US)

martin's hammer knocking at the wicket [18C–19C] (pregnant with twins)

Mr Knap has been there [early 19C] (i.e. 'knapped')

Mr Knap is concerned [early 19C] (i.e. 'knapped')

on the hill [1950s+] (US)

on the nest [20C] (US)

on the stick [1940s+] (orig. Aus.)

on the way [late 16C+]

plunked [20C] (Aus./N.Z.)

podding [late 19C+]

poisoned [late 17C–early 19C; 20C]

preggers [1920s+]

preggy [1920s+]

prego/preggo [1920s+] (Aus.)

priggling [1930s+]

pu the elop [20C] (backslang, 'up the pole')

run to seed [mid-19C]

sewed up/sewn up [mid-19C]

showing [1930s+] (visibly pregnant)

spitting at the tongs [20C] (Ulster)

stung by a serpent [19C]

that way [1930s+] (US)

thickening for something [1950s+]

up the creek (without a paddle) [1930s+] (Aus.)

up the duff [1940s+] (orig. Aus.; from the name of a type of pudding)

up the kite [1990s+]

up the pole [1920s+]

up the spout [early 19C–1920s]

up the stick [1930s+] (orig. Aus.)

up the way [20C] (Aus.)

TO BECOME PREGNANT

burn one's foot [20C] (US)

catch [late 19C+]

click [1930s+]

cut one's leg [late 17C–late 18C]

eat dried apples [20C] (US: i.e. to swell up like dried fruit placed in water)

eat peaches [20C] (US)

eat pumpkin seeds [20C] (US)

fall [late 19C+]

make feet for children's shoes [1930s+] (US Black)

sprain one's ankle [late 18C+] (to become pregnant out of wedlock)

swallow a watermelon seed [20C] (US)

TO BE PREGNANT

have a bun in the oven [1940s+]

have a cookie in the oven [1960s] (US)

have a dumpling on [late 19C]

have a joey in the pouch [1950s–60s] (Aus.)

have an egg in the nest [20C] (US Black)

have a trout in the well [1940s] (Irish)

have a two-legged tympany [late 16C–early 18C]
   (*tympany* = tumour)

have a white swelling [late 18C–early 19C]

have one in the box [late 19C+]

have one's belly full [late 18C]

have one up [1960s]

TO GIVE BIRTH

be cured of a tympany with two heels [late 16C–
   early 18C] (*tympany* = tumour)

drop [mid-17C+]

drop a frog [1970s] (US)

drop one's load [late 19C]

fall to pieces [late 19C+]

go down [1900s–20s]

go to pieces [mid-19C–1900s]

pip [1970s]

drop a frog

piss bones [late 19C–1900s]
piss children [late 19C–1900s]
piss hard [late 19C–1900s]
plunk a baby [20C] (Aus./N.Z.)
pod [late 19C+]
pop (off) [1950s+]
slip a joey [20C] (Aus.)
whelp [late 19C–1900s]

ORAL FUNCTIONS

ORAL FLATULENCE

TO BELCH

burp [1930s+] (orig. US)

break a pudding [20C] (Irish)

gurk [1920s+]

let one fly [1970s+] (US campus)

let one go [1970s+] (US campus)

let one off [1970s+] (US campus)

let one rip [1970s+] (US campus)

repeat [late 19C+]

○○○○○○○○○○○○○○○○○○○○○○○○○○○○○○○○○
Vomiting copiously and violently

boil off the stomach [20C] (US)

bring one's heart up [late 19C]

bring one's ring up [1970s]

cough up one's guts [19C+]

spew one's guts [1930s+]

spew one's ring [1960s+]

throw up one's boots [20C] (US)

throw up one's heels/throw up one's toes
[20C] (US)

vomit up one's toenails [20C] (US)

○○○○○○○○○○○○○○○○○○○○○○○○○○○○○○○○○

BELCHES

beer's talking [20C] (used to excuse a belch)

burp [1930s+]

cheeser [19C]

Raquel Welch [20C] (rhy. sl. 'belch')

repeaters [20C] (Aus.)

vurp [1990s] (a belch that brings up a small quantity of
stomach juice)

Wyatt Earp [20C] (rhy. sl. 'burp')

VOMIT AND VOMITING

TO VOMIT

air one's paunch [1930s–40s] (US)

blow [1930s+]

blow chow [1930s+] (US)

blow chunks [1930s+]

blow one's cookies [1930s+]

blow one's lunch [1950s+] (US)

boke/boak [1990s+]

bring up [early 18C+]

calf [20C] (US)

call for ralph [1960s+]

calve [mid-19C] (US)

cascade [17C–mid-19C]

cast up one's accounts [17C–19C]

cat (up) [late 18C]

chuck (a) seven [1970s+]

chuck one's biscuits [1990s]

chuck the dummy [late 19C]

cotch [1970s+] (S. Afr.)

cough (it) [late 19C+] (orig US)

cough up [late 19C+]

○○○○○○○○○○○○○○○○○○○○○○○○○○○○○○○○
To vomit in rhyming slang
tom and dick [1970s+] ('be sick')

Uncle Dick [1970s+] ('be sick')

Wallace and Gromit [1990s+]

○○○○○○○○○○○○○○○○○○○○○○○○○○○○○○○○

○○○○○○○○○○○○○○○○○○○○○○○○○○○○○○○○
Parking the custard: the upper classes at play
call for bill [1960s+] (UK society)

call for hughie [1960s+] (UK society)

park a custard [1970s+] (UK society)

○○○○○○○○○○○○○○○○○○○○○○○○○○○○○○○○

speak Welsh

cry hughie [1960s+]

do a cat [mid–late 19C]

dump one's load [1960s+]

flash the hash [late 18C+] (orig. UK Und.)

flay the fox [mid-17C–late 18C]

flip one's cookies [1950s+]

give up one's halfpenny [late 17C–late 18C]

heave [20C]

holler New York [1960s+] (US)

jack up [1990s] (US)

jerk the cat [early 17C]

kotch [1970s+] (S. Afr.)

launch one's lunch [1990s]

lose [mid-19C+] (US)

paint the town red [late 19C+]

park a leopard [1990s] (from the varicoloured nature of what is brought up)

park a tiger [1990s]

pop one's cake [1920s] (US)

pop one's cookies [1930s+] (US)

pump bilge [20C] (US)

pump ship [late 18C+]

ride the buick [1960s+] (US)

shit [late 19C]

shit through one's teeth [late 18C+]

shoot one's mouth off [mid-19C+]

shoot the cat [late 18C+]

sling a cat [19C]

speak Welsh [1990s+]

spill one's breakfast [20C]

split a gut [1950s]

throw [20C]

throw a seven [late 19C+]

throw one's cookies [1960s+] (US)

throw up [late 19C+]

throw up one's accounts [mid–late 18C]

○○○○○○○○○○○○○○○○○○○○○○○○○○○○○○○○○○○○
Maritime vomiting

feed the fishes [20C] (US; to vomit over the side of a ship)

feed the goldfish [20C] (US; to vomit over the side of a ship)

feed the kippers [20C] (US; to vomit over the side of a ship)

○○○○○○○○○○○○○○○○○○○○○○○○○○○○○○○○○○○○

toss a reverse lunch [1970s+] (N.Z.)

toss one's lollies [1980s+] (N.Z.)

toss the tiger [1960s+] (N.Z.)

unspit [late 19C]

unswallow [1930s]

upchuck [1920s+] (orig. US)

vom [1960s+]

whip the cat [17C]

whoops [1920s+] (US)

TEEN AND CAMPUS VOMITING

blow one's doughnuts [1970s+] (US campus)

blow one's groceries [1970s+] (US campus)

call the dogs [1990s] (US campus)

cheese [1980s+] (US campus)

chew the cheese [1980s+] (US campus)

chummy [1980s+] (US campus)

chum the fish [1980s+] (US campus; SE *chum*, to throw ground bait into the water to attract fish)

chunk [1980s+] (US campus)

flash (ones' cookies) [1970s+] (US campus)

fred [1980s+] (US campus)

hack [1970s] (US campus)

lose it [1970s+] (US campus)

lose one's doughnuts [1940s+] (US campus)

reverse gears [1980s+] (US teen)

shoot one's cookies [1970s+] (US campus)

spread a technicolour rainbow [1970s+] (US campus)

toss [1950s+] (US campus)

toss one's cookies [1970s+] (orig. US campus)

water buffalo [1980s+] (US campus)

yuck (up) [1960s+] (US campus/teen)

CHUCKLING AND CHUNDERING: VOMITING À L'AUSTRALIENNE

burp (a rainbow) [1960s+] (Aus.)

call [1990s] (Aus.)

call Charles [1960s+] (Aus.)

call for herb [1960s+] (Aus.)

drive the porcelain bus

chuck [mid-19C+] (orig. US/Aus.)

chuckle [1960s+] (Aus./Queensland)

chunder [1950s+] (orig. Aus.)

go (for) the big spit [1950s+] (Aus.)

hurl [1960s+] (Aus./S. Afr.)

laugh at the ground [1960s+] (Aus.)

lose [mid-19C+] (US)

○○○○○○○○○○○○○○○○○○○○○○○○○○○○○○○○○○○○○○○

Making love to the lav:
vomiting in the toilet bowl

drive the bus [1970s+]

drive the porcelain bus [1970s+] (US campus)

make love to the lav [1960s+] (Aus.)

make love to the porcelain goddess [1960s+] (US campus)

pray to the porcelain goddess [1960s+] (US campus)

ride the porcelain bus [1960s+] (US campus)

talk to Ralph on the big white telephone [1970s+] (orig. US campus)

talk to the big white phone [1970s+] (orig. US campus)

○○○○○○○○○○○○○○○○○○○○○○○○○○○○○○○○○○○○○○○

lose a dinner [1950s+] (Aus.)

lose a meal [1940s+] (Aus.)

lose one's lunch [1940s+] (Aus./US)

make a sale [1930s+] (Aus.)

perk (up) [1960s] (Aus.)

play the whale [1960s–70s] (Aus.)

sell out [20C] (Aus.)

throw a map [1940s+] (Aus.)

throw a seven [late 19C+]

throw one's cookies [1960s+] (US)

throw one's voice [1960s+] (Aus.)

throw sixers [20C] (Aus.)

up and under [1950s+] (Aus.; rhy. sl. 'chunder')

yodel [1960s+] (Aus.)

ONOMATOPOEIC

barf [1940s+] (mainly US campus)

bison [1980s+] (US campus)

boag [1980s+] (US campus)

boot [1970s+] (US campus)

buick [1960s+] (US)

burk [20C] (US)

chirp [mid-19C+] (US campus)

earl [1960s+] (US)

hoop [1980s] (US)

kak [1960s+] (US)

New York [1950s] (W.I.)

ook [1990s] (US campus)

ralph [1970s+] (US campus)

woof [1970s+] (US campus)

yak/yack [1990s] (US campus)

yawp [late 19C+]

yoff [1990s+]

yuke [1990s] (US campus)

zuke [1980s+] (US campus)

THE ACT OF VOMITING

big spit/long spit [1960s+] (Aus.)

catting [late 18C+]

dump [1950s+] (drugs; the vomiting that may follow an
   injection of heroin)

good stick [1950s+] (drugs; the short-lived bout of
   vomiting that can follow an injection of heroin)

grand slam [1990s+] (simultaneous vomiting and
   defecation)

happy returns [late 19C–1920s] (Aus.)

heave(-ho) [1940s+] (US)

hughie/huey [1950s+] (Aus.)

instant boot camp [20C] (US campus)

lunch gut [1950s+] (drugs; the vomiting that may
   follow an injection of heroin)

multicoloured yawn [1960s+] (orig. Aus.)

perk [1960s] (Aus.)

stripey laugh [1990s+]

technicolor cough [1960s+] (orig. Aus.)

technicolor spit [1960s+] (orig. Aus.)

technicolour yawn [1960s+] (orig. Aus.)

throw [20C]

whip o'will [1960s+] (Aus.)

yell [1960s+]

THE STUFF ITSELF

barf [1960s+]

boak [20C] (Ulster)

boke [20C] (Ulster)

chuck [20C]

chunder [1960s+]

cookies [1920s+]

cotch [1970s+] (S. Afr.)

liquid laugh [1960s+] (orig. Aus.)

lunch [1910s+] (US)

pavement pizza [1980s+] (Aus.: a pile of vomit)

tummy mud [1990s]

vom [1960s+]

BLOOD, SWEAT... AND SPITTLE

BLOOD

bleed [late 19C–1900s]

bordeaux [mid-19C–1900s]

carmine [early–mid-19C]

claret [early 17C+]

crunt [1950s–60s] (US Black; dried blood)

Dutch pink [19C]

goo [20C]

goo-goo [20C] (orig. US)

gravy [mid-18C+]

juice [20C] (orig.US)

ketchup [1940s–70s] (US)

October [mid-19C] (*October* ale, a type of strong beer)

red gravy [1940s] (US Black)

red ink [mid-19C]

°°°°°°°°°°°°°°°°°°°°°°°°°°°°°°°°°°°°
To bleed

bleed like a (stuck) pig [17C+] (to bleed heavily,
to lose a good deal of blood)

claret [early 19C] (orig. boxing)

peel the bark [19C] (boxing; to draw blood)

tap [mid–late 19C] (to draw blood from a victim's
nose)

°°°°°°°°°°°°°°°°°°°°°°°°°°°°°°°°°°°°

MUCUS

SNOT

boo [1990s] (US)

booie [1920s+] (Aus.)

pease pudding hot [20C] (rhy. sl. 'snot')

snot [18C]

BOGEYS

bogey [1930s+]

booger [late 19C+] (US)

boogie [late 19C+] (US)

bovey [1920s+] (Aus.)

bugaboo [1910s+] (W.I.)

cootie [1970s] (US juv.)

Jimmy Logie [1950s] (rhy. sl. 'bogey')

Polish handball [1960s] (US gay)

○○○○○○○○○○○○○○○○○○○○○○○○○○○○○○○
Eye boogers

eye booger [1980s+] (US campus)

gravy-eyed [late 18C–19C] (having mucus-filled
eyes)

○○○○○○○○○○○○○○○○○○○○○○○○○○○○○○○

°°°°°°°°°°°°°°°°°°°°°°°°°°°°°°°°°°°°°°
Nose-picking and -blowing

sling [mid–late 19C] (to blow one's nose with one's fingers)

sling a snot [late 19C] (to blow one's nose with one's fingers)

winkle-fishing [1910s–20s] (the act of nose-picking)

°°°°°°°°°°°°°°°°°°°°°°°°°°°°°°°°°°°°°°

°°°°°°°°°°°°°°°°°°°°°°°°°°°°°°°°°°°°°°
Dewdrops and dilberries

candlestick [20C] (Irish; a drop of mucus running from the nose)

dewdrop [20C] (a drop of mucus lodged at the opening of a nostril and hanging there before removal)

dilberry [mid-19C+] (a piece of nasal mucus dripping from the bottom of the nostril)

lamb's leg [20C] (a piece of mucus running from one's nose)

snailer [1990s] (Irish; a trail of mucus running down the face)

°°°°°°°°°°°°°°°°°°°°°°°°°°°°°°°°°°°°°°

SPITTLE and PHLEGM

SPITTLE

drool [mid-19C–1940s] (US)

LUMPS OF PHLEGM

clam [1970s+] (a lump of phlegm)

docker's omelette [1990s+]

gobshite [late 19C–1910s] (US; an expectorated wad of
   tobacco)

gold watch [1990s+]

gollier/gollywer [20C] (Irish)

gollion [20C] (Aus.)

golly [1960s+] (Aus.)

gonga [1990s+]

goober [1960s+] (US)

goob [1960s+] (US)

gooey [20C] (Aus.)

hawker [1970s+] (US)

hocker [1960s] (US teen)

honker [1980s+] (US)

looey [1970s+] (US)

lieuy [1970s+] (US)

looie [1970s+] (US)

candlestick

○○○○○○○○○○○○○○○○○○○○○○○○○○○○○○○○○○
Greenies and yellow backs
greenie [1980s+] (US teen)

green one [1990s+]

yellow back [1940s+] (Aus.)

○○○○○○○○○○○○○○○○○○○○○○○○○○○○○○○○○○

loogie [1980s+] (US)

louie [1970s+]

lunger [1930s+]

oyster [late 18C+]

TO SPIT

flob [1930s+] (mainly juv.)

gob [late 19C+]

golly [1930s+] (Aus.)

goo/goob [20C] (Aus.)

have donkey in one's throat [late 19C] (to have
   phlegm caught in one's throat)

hawker [1970s+] (US)

hoick [20C] (Aus.)

hork [1990s] (US)

slag [1960s+] (Aus.)

spit amber [late 19C] (US; to spit while chewing
   tobacco)

spit cotton [early 19C–1940s] (drugs; to spit white
   balls of spittle while under the influence of
   amphetamines)

spit sixpences/spit white broth [late 18C–late 19C]
   (to spit out small gobbets of white mucus)

yock [1990s+]

SWEAT

arse vinegar [1990s+] (sweat that accumulates between the cleft of the buttocks)

arsevoir [1990s+] (a place at the top of anal cleft in which sweat gathers)

biffin [1990s] (sweat secreted during intercourse)

bum juice [1990s] (sweat that gathers between the buttocks)

elbow grease [late 17C–18C]

funk [1950s+] (US Black; sweat generated during sex)

malaria [1980s] (US Black)

muck-sweat [early 19C+]

TO SWEAT

bleed [20C] (US)

do a swelter [mid–late 19C]

piss one's tallow [17C–19C]

sweat cobs [1950s+]

sweat like a bull [late 19C+]

sweat like a nigger (at election) [1900s–50s]

sweat like a pig [late 19C+]

THE BODY MALODOROUS

TO SMELL

bottle [20C] (rhy. sl. *bottle of drink*, stink)

fogue [1920s–1930s] (N.Z.)

fonk [17C–19C]

honk [1920s+] (orig. Aus.)

honk like a gaggle of geese [1920s+] (Aus.)

hoot [1920s+] (orig. Aus.)

hum [late 19C+]

ming [1970s+] (orig. Scot.)

naar [1980s+] (S. Afr.; Afrikaans, 'nauseating')

niff [1920s+]

pen (and ink) [late 19C+] (rhy. sl. 'stink')

pong [1920s+]

smell like a badger's touch-hole [17C–late 19C]

smell like a ram-goat [20C] (W.I.)

whiff [late 19C+]

whistle [1930s]

SMELLY

cheesy [late 19C+]

Hogan's goat [20C] (US)

mankie/manky [1940s+] (orig. Ling. Fr./Polari)

smell like a ram-goat

niffy [20C]

on the bugle [early 19C+]

on the nose [1940s+] (Aus./N.Z.)

pooey [1930s+] (orig. Aus.)

poofy [1940s+] (juv.)

stanky [1970s+] (orig. US)

BODILY ODOURS

frito toes [1980s+] (US campus; very smelly feet)

parfum de corsage [1920s–30s] (the odour of cosmetics and sweat accruing to a woman participating energetically at a dance)

pits [1990s+] (US campus; body odour)

smell of broken glass [1900s–30s] (a stench of body odour, typically in a sports changing room)

GENITAL ODOURS, MAINLY VAGINAL

chuff chowder [1990s+] (vaginal odour)

clambake [1990s] (US; a smelly vagina)

funk [1950s+] (US Black; the odour of the male or female genitals)

gluepot has come unstuck [late 19C] (said of someone who smells of semen or recent intercourse)

ling [19C] (vaginal odour; from a type of fish)

p.t.a. [1970s+] (US Black; the smelly parts of a woman: *p*ussy, *t*its and *a*rmpits)

queef [1990s] (US; unpleasant-smelling vaginal gas)

wolf pussy [1970s] (US Black; unpleasant vaginal odour)

SPOTS, BOILS AND PIMPLES

acca [1980s+] (Aus.)

boo-boo [1950s+] (US; an acne spot)

chorb [1970s+] (S. Afr. teen)

courage bump [20C] (US)

crater [1980s+]

custards [1920s+]

dohickey [1910s+] (US)

floaters [1950s+]

flying flies [1950s+]

gin-bud [19C] (a facial spot or ulcer resulting from excessive gin-drinking)

goober [1970s+] (US campus; lit. 'peanut')

goopheads [1940s+] (US)

hickey [1950s+] (US)

jack bumps [1960s+] (US)

penny pots [mid-19C–1920s]

pimgenet [late 17C– early 18C]

pip [1950s+]

pluke [20C]

presents [late 19C+]

prick [mid-16C–late 17C]

zilch [1960s+]

zit [1950s+]

oooooooooooooooooooooooooooooooooooo

Spots in rhyming slang

Rhyming with 'boil'

can of oil [late 19C+]

Conan Doyle [late 19C+]

Rhyming with 'spot'

Randolph Scott [20C]

Selina Scott [20C]

oooooooooooooooooooooooooooooooooooo

BODILY MALFUNCTIONS 1:

ILLNESSES (MOST OF THEM VENEREAL)

ILL

bum [late 19C+] (slightly ill)

cheap [late 19C–1920s]

crawly-mawly [mid-19C] (Norfolk dial.)

crook [20C]

crooked [20C]

dangerous [late 19C] (US; seriously ill)

dicky [late 18C+]

done up [late 18C–early 19C]

dopey [19C+] (mildly ill)

green about the gills [late 19C+]

jiggered [mid-19C+] (exhausted)

knocked over [late 19C] (feeling very ill)

lunk [late 19C+] (Scot. *lunkie*, close, sultry)

mendic [1920s+] (Aus.)

∘∘∘∘∘∘∘∘∘∘∘∘∘∘∘∘∘∘∘∘∘∘∘∘∘∘∘∘∘∘∘∘∘∘∘∘∘∘∘
Very sick

sick as a cat [mid–late 19C]

sick as a cushion [late 17C–18C]

sick as a dog [late 17C+]

sick as a horse [late 18C–early 19C]

sick as a rat [19C+]

sick in fourteen languages [late 19C] (US)

∘∘∘∘∘∘∘∘∘∘∘∘∘∘∘∘∘∘∘∘∘∘∘∘∘∘∘∘∘∘∘∘∘∘∘∘∘∘∘

○○○○○○○○○○○○○○○○○○○○○○○○○○○○○○○○○○○○○○
Ill in rhyming slang

Rhyming with 'sick'

bob and dick [1960s+]

bob, harry and dick [late 19C–1900s]

harry, tom and dick/tom, harry and dick [20C]

moby dick [20C]

old mick [late 19C+]

spotted dick [20C]

Rhyming with 'crook'

butcher's hook [20C] (Aus.)

Captain Cook [1950s] (Aus.)

○○○○○○○○○○○○○○○○○○○○○○○○○○○○○○○○○○○○○

mickey [late 19C]

micky [late 19C]

mouldy [mid-19C]

naar [1960s+] (S. Afr.: Afrikaans, 'nauseated')

naughty [1960s+]

peaked [mid–late 19C] (looking ill)

queer [late 18C+]

ragged [1950s+] (Aus.)

scaly [late 18C–mid-19C]

sewed up [mid-19C]

sick as a dog

TO FEEL ILL

crack up [mid-19C+]

crook up [1910s+] (Aus.: to fall ill)

feel funny [early 19C+]

feel like a boiled rag [20C]

feel like a piece of chewed string [20C]

go crook (on) [1910s+] (Aus.)

have the bot [1940s+] (Aus./N.Z.; from the parasitic *bot*fly)

have the miseries [20C] (US Black)

have the pip [late 19C+]

ILLNESSES: A SHORT A–Z

all-over/all-overs [mid-19C+] (an *all-over* feeling of illness)

barcoo [late 19C] (Aus.; sickness caused by the ingestion of fly-polluted food)

barcoo spew [1910s+] (Aus.; severe sickness and dysentery brought on by drinking bad water)

barcoo vomit [1910s+] (Aus.; severe sickness and dysentery brought on by drinking bad water)

○○○○○○○○○○○○○○○○○○○○○○○○○○○○○○○○○○○○
Look like death
look like death eating a sandwich [1940s+]

look like death warmed up [1930s+]

○○○○○○○○○○○○○○○○○○○○○○○○○○○○○○○○○○○○

○○○○○○○○○○○○○○○○○○○○○○○○○○○○○○○○○○○○
One foot in the grave
another clean shirt ought to see you out [1930s+] (N.Z.)

booked [20C] (US; i.e. *booked* into heaven)

have a notice to quit [early–mid-19C]

○○○○○○○○○○○○○○○○○○○○○○○○○○○○○○○○○○○○

Belyando spew [late 19C–1900s] (Aus.; a rural sickness)

bug [1910s+] (orig. US)

collywobbles [mid-19C] (a feeling of sickness in the stomach)

cotch [1970s+] (S. Afr.)

crank [late 16C–early 17C] (epilepsy)

dose [20C] (Ulster; a bad attack of an illness)

feeling of oaks [late 17C–early 18C] (sea-sickness)

gollywobbles [1940s+] (US; a feeling of sickness in the stomach)

green death [1960s–70s] (US campus; sickness caused by student canteen food)

kwaal [1960s+] (S. Afr.; Afrikaans, 'complaint')

lackanooky [1940s+] (US; ill-health caused by lack of sexual activity)

oony [20C] (Aus.; sea-sickness)

pip [late 19C+] (from a type of poultry disease)

wamble/the wambles [late 17C–18C] (a feeling of nausea or queasiness)

wog [1930s–70s] (Aus.)

DEPRESSION

bear [1940s+] (US Black)

black ass [1940s–60s] (US)

black dog [early 19C+]

black rot [mid-19C] (US)

blahs [1960s+] (Aus./US)

blue devils [18C]

blues [mid-18C+]

colly-molly [17C] (play on SE *melancholy*)

darks [late 18C]

dismals [mid-18C–mid-19C]

downer [1970s+]

droop(s) [20C]

dumps [late 17C+]

English disease [18C–19C]

fol-de-rol [late 19C] (US; temporary low spirits; lit. 'trifle')

funk [mid-18C+]

glooms [1910s–70s]

graums [1950s] (US)

headstaggers [20C]

horrors [mid-18C+]

hypo [18C–19C] (a feeling of mild depression)

joes [1910s+] (rhy. sl. *joe blakes*, shakes)

low [1970s+]

low cotton [1940s+]

moody [1930s+]

mubble-fubbles [late 16C–mid-17C] (from SE *mumble* and *fumble*)

sniffles [1900s] (US)

VENEREAL DISEASE

bone-ache [late 16C–early 17C]

brophys [1950s+] (Irish)

bube [early 17C–18C]

burner [mid-18C–19C]

Chinese rot [1940s–60s] (US)

clapier [16C] (French, 'venereal bubo')

clapoire [16C] (French, 'venereal bubo')

cock-rot [1980s+] (US)

crinkum [early 17C–late 18C]

crud [1950s+] (US)

dog [1940s]

dose [late 19C+]

fire [early 18C–19C]

flame [19C]

flapdragon [late 17C–late 18C]

garden gout [early 19C]

gentleman's [20C] (W.I.)

gift that keeps on giving [1980s+] (US campus)

glim [mid–late 19C]

glimmer [16C–17C]

haddums/had 'em [late 17C–late 18C] (from the phrase 'been at had 'em and come home by Clapham', i.e. 'the clap')

handicap [20C] (rhy. sl. 'clap')

kertever cartzo [mid-19C] (Ling. Fr. *cattivo cazzo*, bad cock)

load [19C+] (orig. Aus.)

lobstertails [1940s–60s] (US Black)

measles [mid-19C]

nap [late 17C–early 18C]

noli me tangere [17C–19C] (Scot.; Latin, 'touch-me-not')

oozing scabs [1980s+] (US campus)

pox [16C+]

sauce [late 18C–early 19C]

scalder [17C]

scrubbado [mid-17C–early 18C] (*scrub* = itch)

scrud [1930s+] (US, orig. milit.)

stick [late 19C+]

token [18C]

Venus's curse [19C]

whites [late 17C+]

THE POX IN RHYMING SLANG

band in the box [1960s+]

boots and socks [20C] (Aus.)

cardboard box [1970s+]

coachman on the box [20C]

Collie Knox [1960s+]

jack [1950s+] (Aus.)

jack in the box [late 19C+]

nervo and knox [1970s+]

Reverend Ronald Knox [1950s]

royal docks [20C]

shoes and sox [20C]

Surrey docks [1970s]

Tilbury docks [late 19C+]

Whitehaven docks [1970s]

GONORRHOEA

applause [1990s] (US Black; playing on 'clap')

blue balls [1930s+] (US)

botch [1960s] (US; lit. an eruptive sore)

bullhead clap [1940s–50s] (US; a very bad case of
   gonorrhoea)

clap [late 16C+] (Old French *clapoir*, a venereal bubo)

clapper [mid-18C+] (US)

○○○○○○○○○○○○○○○○○○○○○○○○○○○○○○○○
Double doses

double event [late 19C] (a simultaneous bout of
   syphilis and gonorrhoea)

full hand [1940s+] (Aus.; a simultaneous bout of
   syphilis and gonorrhoea)

○○○○○○○○○○○○○○○○○○○○○○○○○○○○○○○○

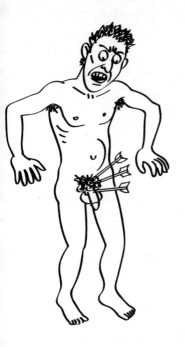

cupid's itch

claps [late 16C+]

cupid's itch [1930s+] (US)

drip [1960s+] (from the discharge produced in sufferers)

dripper [late 17C–18C]

garden gout [early 19C] (i.e. Covent *Garden*, London)

gentleman's complaint [1920s+] (W.I.)

gleet [1940s+] (Aus.; lit. 'slime, purulent matter')

glue [late 19C+]

goodyear [17C] (French sl. *gouge*, a slut)

horse (and trap) [1960s+] (rhy. sl. 'clap')

little casino [1960s+] (US; i.e. gonorrhoea as the 'lesser' form of venereal disease)

nine-day blues [20C] (the incubation period for gonorrhoea after the initial sexual contact)

strain [1970s+] (US)

whites [19C] (from the colour of the accompanying vaginal discharge)

∘∘∘∘∘∘∘∘∘∘∘∘∘∘∘∘∘∘∘∘∘∘∘∘∘∘∘∘∘∘∘∘∘∘∘
A venereal tour of Britain

Barnwell ague [mid-17C–mid-19C]

Covent Garden ague [17C–late 18C]

Covent Garden gout [late 17C]

Drury Lane ague [mid-18C–late 19C]

Piccadilly cramp [18C]

Scotch fiddle [18C–19C]

Tetbury portion [late 18C–early 19C] ('a cunt and a clap': i.e. sexual intercourse followed by a dose of venereal disease)

Welsh fiddle [18C–19C]

Winchester goose [16C–early 17C] (from the diocese of *Winchester* which had jurisdiction over the brothels of Southwark)

∘∘∘∘∘∘∘∘∘∘∘∘∘∘∘∘∘∘∘∘∘∘∘∘∘∘∘∘∘∘∘∘∘∘∘

Gallic nastiness

blow with a French faggot stick [late 17C–early 18C] (referring to the loss of the nose through the effects of syphilis)

French cannibal [early 17C]

French crown [late 17C–18C]

French disease [late 16C–late 18C]

French goods [late 17C–18C]

French gout [late 17C–18C]

Frenchman [19C]

French marbles [late 16C]

French measles [early 17C]

French pox [early 16C–late 18C]

SYPHILIS

boogie-woogie [20C] (US South)

copper pox [1920s–1930s] (from the folk belief that holding two copper coins beneath one's tongue during intercourse, would cause one's partner to become infected with syphilis)

Cupid's measles [1940s–50s] (US)

deuce [17C+]

grincam/grincom/grincome/grincum [17C]

jack [20C]

Syphilis in rhyming slang

Rhyming with 'syph'

bang and biff [20C]

lover's tiff [20C]

will's whiff [20C]

∘∘∘∘∘∘∘∘∘∘∘∘∘∘∘∘∘∘∘∘∘∘∘∘∘∘∘∘∘∘∘∘∘∘

old dog [1930s–50s] (US)

old joe [1910s+] (US)

old ral/old rale [late 19C–1960s] (US)

pip [late 19C+]

scabbado [17C]

syph/sypho [1910s+] (Aus.)

∘∘∘∘∘∘∘∘∘∘∘∘∘∘∘∘∘∘∘∘∘∘∘∘∘∘∘∘∘∘∘∘∘∘∘

Neapolitan nastiness

Naples canker [16C]

Neapolitan bone-ache [16C]

Neapolitan button [16C]

Neapolitan favour [16C]

Neapolitan scab [16C]

Neapolitan scurf [16C]

∘∘∘∘∘∘∘∘∘∘∘∘∘∘∘∘∘∘∘∘∘∘∘∘∘∘∘∘∘∘∘∘∘∘∘

VENEREAL BUBOS

blue balls [20C]

blue boar [late 18C–mid-19C]

blue board [20C]

blue boy [18C–19C]

dumb watch [late 18C]

French pig [late 17C–18C] (the syphilitic pustule or bubo)

pintle-blossom [18C–1900s]

poulain [late 18C–early 19C] (French)

INFECTED WITH A VENEREAL DISEASE

between the two Ws [mid-19C] (i.e. between wind and water)

burned [late 17C–19C]

clapped(-up) [17C+]

clappy [1960s+]

clawed off [late 17C–late 18C]

dosed (up) [late 19C+]

fly-blown [late 19C] (suspected of carrying a venereal disease: *flyblow* = gossip)

frenchified [late 17C–19C]

have a bad cold [mid-19C–1910s]

have been after the girls [mid–late 19C]

have one's tail on fire [late 17C–early 18C]

high [late 19C] (used of prostitutes: lit. 'slightly gone off')

hot [late 17C–19C]

hot-tailed [late 17C–early 18C]

in for the plate [late 18C–early 19C] (horses that qualify for the main race, or *plate*, have already won the 'heat': symptoms of venereal disease include inflammation, i.e. *heat*)

in pickle [late 17C–18C] (the contemporary cure for venereal disease involved sitting in a 'sweating tub')

jacked up [20C] (Aus.)

lit up [late 19C+] (Aus.)

one of the knights [1970s] (gay: the disease attacks one's 'sword')

peppered (off) [late 17C–18C] (very badly infected with a venereal disease)

piled for French velvet [17C]

placket-stung [mid–late 19C] (*placket* = vagina)

posed (up) [late 17C+]

poxed(-up) [late 17C+]

scalded [19C]

○○○○○○○○○○○○○○○○○○○○○○○○○○○○○○○○○○○

Spanish nastiness

Spanish gout [late 17C–early 19C]

Spanish needle [late 17C–early 19C]

Spanish pox [late 17C–18C]

○○○○○○○○○○○○○○○○○○○○○○○○○○○○○○○○○○○

○○○○○○○○○○○○○○○○○○○○○○○○○○○○○○○○○○○
Pissing broken glass

pissing broken glass [1960s+]

pissing out of a dozen holes [late 19C+]
(infected with syphilis, from the rotting of the
penis)

pissing pins and needles [late 18C–early 19C]

pissing pure cream [late 19C] (infected with
gonorrhoea, from the discharge that
accompanies the disease)

○○○○○○○○○○○○○○○○○○○○○○○○○○○○○○○○○○○

shot between wind and water [late 17C–19C] (referring
to a ship shot in the side in an area sometimes above the
water and sometimes submerged, where a shot is
particularly damaging)

sunburnt [late 16C–early 17C]

TO CATCH A VENEREAL DISEASE

break one's shins against Covent Garden rails [late
18C–early 19C]

burn one's poker [19C–1900s]

cop a dose [1940s+]

cop a packet [1930s+]

gash [1990s]

pissing out of a dozen holes

get a knob [1950s–60s] (orig. milit.)

get anything [late 17C+]

get a packet [1930s+]

get it [mid-19C+]

have a packet [1930s+]

pass through the fire [19C]

pick up a nail [20C] (W.I.)

take French lessons [20C]

TO INFECT SOMEONE WITH A VENEREAL DISEASE

burn [16C: 20C]

clap [late 16C+]

load up [1930s+] (Aus./N.Z.)

scald [17C–late 19C]

set on fire [17C–18C]

shoot between wind and water [late 17C–1900s]

swinge off [17C–18C] (*swinge* = have sex with)

tip someone the token [18C] (*token* = a venereal disease)

○○○○○○○○○○○○○○○○○○○○○○○○○○○○○○○○○○
Venereal discharge

dripper [late 17C–18C]

running horse [late 18C–mid-19C] (rhy. sl. *horse and trap.* clap)

running nag [late 18C–mid-19C]

running range [1920s–50s] (US Black)

○○○○○○○○○○○○○○○○○○○○○○○○○○○○○○○○○○

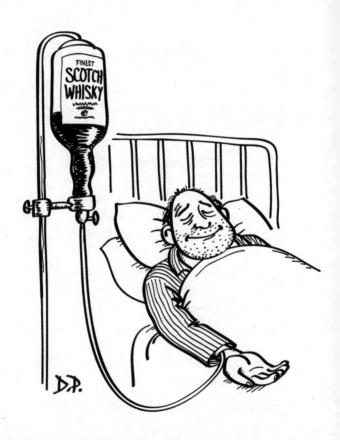

BODILY

MALFUNCTIONS 2:

DRUNKENNESS

DRUNK

TIPSY

all right [20C]

altogethery [early 19C–1930s] (UK society)

bonkers [1940s+]

buzzed [1960s+]

chucked [late 19C]

dithered [1920s+] (Aus.)

fettled [19C]

flared [1960s+] (Can.)

fresh/freshish [mid-19C]

funny [mid-18C]

hickey [late 18C+]

horrid [late 18C]

how-come-ye-so [18C]

in a merry pin [late 18C–early 19C]

kisky [mid-19C] (rhy. sl. 'whisky')

lekker [mid-19C+] (S. Afr.; Dutch, 'pleasant, tasty')

muckibus [mid-18C–mid-19C]

off nicely [19C]

off the nail [early 19C]

on [late 19C]

pertish [mid-18C–early 19C]

pleasant [mid-19C]

rosy [20C]

rum/room [mid-16C–early 19C]

slathered [1920s+]

○○○○○○○○○○○○○○○○○○○○○○○○○○○○○○○○○
Half-rinsed

flatch-kennurd [mid-19C] (backslang. 'half
  drunk')

half in the bag/half in the wrapper [1940s+]
  (orig. US)

half-canned [1920s+]

half-cocked [20C]

half-fonged [1940s+] (N.Z.)

half-high [20C] (US)

half-nelson [1920s]

half-off, half-on [late 19C]

half-pissed [20C]

half-rats [late 19C]

half-rinsed [1910s+] (Aus./N.Z.)

half-screwed [mid-19C+]

half-slewed [early 19C+]

half-tore [20C] (Ulster)

madza beargured [mid-19C+] (Ling. Fr./Polari:
  lit. 'half drunk')

○○○○○○○○○○○○○○○○○○○○○○○○○○○○○○○○○

slightly tightly [late 19C]

snuffy [mid-19C]

sucky [late 17C–18C]

sweet [1940s] (W.I.)

taking it easy [19C]

tiddled [1920s+]

tiddley/tiddy [mid-19C+]

titley [mid-19C+]

toasted [1970s+]

winged/wing'd [mid-19C]

A DRUNKEN A–Z

A

about right [19C+]

addled [18C+]

afloat [early 19C+]

airlocked [20C] (Ulster)

all in [20C]

among the philistines [late 17C–19C]

Appleton talking/Fernandez talking [20C] (W.I.; said of a person who is drunk, from the brand names of popular rums)

ass on backwards [20C]

away with the band [20C] (Ulster)

ass on backwards

B

badered [1980s] (from the RAF's 'legless' ace. Sir Douglas *Bader*)

bagged [19C+]

balmy [mid–late 19C]

bang-up [early 19C+]

barrelled [1910s+] (US)

be-argured [mid-19C–1900s] (i.e. argumentative)

been in the sun [late 18C–late 19C]

ben-bowsy [late 16C–early 17C]

biffy [20C]

○○○○○○○○○○○○○○○○○○○○○○○○○○○○○○○○○
Beery and boozy:
drink-related words from A to B

aled up [20C]

alkied [1940s+]

all keyhole [mid-19C+] (punning on *alcohol*)

beered up [1930s+] (US)

beery [mid-19C+]

bevvied (up) [1930s+]

boosy [mid-16C+]

boozed [mid-19C+]

boozed up [late 19C+]

boozy [mid-16C+]

bouzy [mid-16C+]

bowsy [late 17C]

bubbed [19C] (*bub* = strong drink)

budgy [mid-19C]

buffed [19C]

buffy [mid-19C]

○○○○○○○○○○○○○○○○○○○○○○○○○○○○○○○○○

Brahms and Liszt

Rhyming with 'drunk'

elephant's (trunk) [mid-19C+]

jumbo's trunk [late 19C]

Rhyming with 'pissed'

Adrian (Quist) [1970s+] (Aus.)

booed and hissed [1980s]

Brahms and Liszt [1920s+]

hit and missed [1960s+]

Lilian Gished [1950s–60s]

Lloyd's (List) [20C]

Mozart and Liszt [1920s+]

Oliver Twist [20C]

Schindler's (List) [1990s]

Rhyming with 'plastered'

lord and mastered [20C]

○○

binged (up) [20C]

bingoed [1920s+] (UK society)

blah [1930s+]

bleary [20C]

blocked [1950s+]

○○○○○○○○○○○○○○○○○○○○○○○○○○○○○○○○○○○○○○
Bug-eyed

boss-eyed [mid-19C+]

bug-eyed [20C]

bung-eyed [mid-19C+]

cock-eyed [early 19C+]

cross-eyed [20C]

moon-eyed [18C+] (US)

ory-eyed [late 19C+] (US)

pie-eyed [20C]

popeyed [20C]

pot-eyed [1900s]

squiffy-eyed [late 19C+]

wall-eyed [1920s–30s] (US)

○○○○○○○○○○○○○○○○○○○○○○○○○○○○○○○○○○○○○

blootered [1970s+]

blue [early 19C+] (US/Aus.)

blued [mid-19C]

bluggy [mid-19C–1920s] (US; mispron. of 'bloody')

boiling [late 19C] (US)

bollixed (up) [20C]

bosky [early 18C–mid-19C]

bullaphants [20C] (Irish)

bullshit [1980s+]

bummed [20C]

bummed out [1960s+]

bumpsie/bumpsy [early–mid-17C]

bung [18C–1900s] (Scot.)

bungy [mid-18C]

bunned [1900s–20s] (US)

C

cabbaged [1990s]

candy [mid-18C–early 19C] (mainly Anglo-Irish)

cannon/canon [mid-19C]

cap-sick [early 17C]

carrying a load [20C]

cast [1930s+] (Irish/N.Z.)

clinched [20C]

cocked [20C] (US)

coguey [19C]

columbered [early 17C]

cooked [1930s+] (US)

coopered [late 19C]

corkscrewed [1910s]

cropsick [late 17C–18C]

cup-shaken [early–mid-17C]

○○○○○○○○○○○○○○○○○○○○○○○○○○○○○○○○○○○○○
Corned and juiced:
drink-related words from C to L

chateaued [1980s+] (UK society: punning on the
names of clarets and on *shattered*)

corned [late 18C–19C] (from the use of *corn* in the
distillation of spirits)

drinky [19C] (US)

ginned (up) [early 19C; 20C]

groggy [mid 19C+]

half-shaved [early–mid-19C] (US: *shave* = a drink)

juiced (up) [1940s+] (orig. US)

laced [1980s+] (US)

likkered [mid-19C+] (US)

liquefied [1930s+]

liquored (up) [1920s+] (US)

lush [early 19C+]

lushed [19C+]

lushed up [1920s+]

lushy [early 19C–1940s]

○○○○○○○○○○○○○○○○○○○○○○○○○○○○○○○○○○○○

Dizzy and fluffy:
confusion-related words from A to H

all at sea [late 19C+]

bemused (with beer) [mid-19C]

concerned [late 18C–mid-19C]

dizzy [18C]

dopey [19C+]

dozed [20C] (Ulster; very drunk)

fluffed [mid-19C]

fluffy [late 19C]

flummoxed [mid-19C+]

flustered [late 17C–19C]

fog-bound [1920s–30s]

fogged [mid-19C+]

foggy [early–mid-19C]

foxed [early 17C–late 18C]

fuddled [late 17C+]

fuzzed [late 17C–early 18C]

fuzzy [late 18C+]

having bread and cheese in one's head
[mid-17C–mid-18C]

hazy [mid-19C]

●●●●●●●●●●●●●●●●●●●●●●●●●●●●●●●●●●●

D

diked up/dyked up [1900s]

dinged out [1960s] (US)

dipsy [1970s] (US)

disguised [mid-16C–mid-19C]

doped (out)/doped up [20C] (US)

down by the head [19C]

draped [1940s]

dronk [1960s+] (S. Afr.)

drop-in-his-eye [late 17C–18C]

drunked up/drunked out [1940s+] (US)

dry [20C]

high as Lindbergh

E

eyes set at eight in the morning [early 17C]

eyes set in one's head [early 17C]

○○○○○○○○○○○○○○○○○○○○○○○○○○○○○○○○○
Elevated and exalted

elevated [early 17C–late 19C; 1940s–60s]

exalted [mid-17C–mid-18C] (slightly drunk)

flying blind [20C]

flying high [20C]

high [17C+]

high as a cat's back [mid-19C+] (US)

high as a fiddler's fist [1950s–60s] (US)

high as a Georgia pine [1930s–40s] (US Black; very drunk)

high as a kite [1930s+] (very drunk)

high as Lindbergh [1930s–40s] (US)

high as ninety [mid-19C] (US)

in one's altitudes [17C–late 18C]

in orbit [1970s+]

○○○○○○○○○○○○○○○○○○○○○○○○○○○○○○○○○

F

faded [1980s+]

fallen off the wagon [20C]

far gone [late 19C+] (very drunk)

flag of defiance is out [late 17C–early 19C]

flaked [1910s+]

flakers [1950s+] (orig. naut.)

flako [1950s+]

floozled [1990s+]

flush [19C]

fly-blown/fly-blowed [late 19C]

fonged (up) [1940s+] (N.Z.)

forteyed [1990s+] (US Black: *forty* = a large bottle of beer)

fox-drunk [early 17C] ('drunk but still cunning')

frazzled (out) [1980s+]

frustrated [20C]

fucked up [1970s+]

full [1920s+] (orig. Aus./N.Z.)

G

gaga/gugga [1920s+]

geezed [1900s–10s] (US)

gesuip [1980s] (S. Afr.: Afrikaans *suip*. to drink. used of an
    animal)

get on [1960s] (US Black)

○○○○○○○○○○○○○○○○○○○○○○○○○○○○○○○○○○○

Glorious and glowing:
positively drunk words from A to G

above par [19C]

at rest [19C]

cheerio [1930s+] (S. Afr.)

cheery [18C+]

chipper/chippy [late 19C+] (orig. US)

chirping merry [late 17C–early 19C]

feeling funny [20C]

feeling good [1920s+]

feeling no pain [1920s+]

feeling right royal [late 19C+]

fired up [19C]

gay [19C–1900s]

geed-up [1920s–70s] (US)

giffed [1970s+] (t.*g.i.f.*, thank *g*od *i*t's *F*riday)

glad [19C+]

glorious [late 18C–mid-19C] (very drunk)

glowing [19C]

○○○○○○○○○○○○○○○○○○○○○○○○○○○○○○○○○○○

●●●●●●●●●●●●●●●●●●●●●●●●●●●●●●●●●●●●

Gassed and plastered:
words from World War I

gassed [1910s+]

half-gassed [1910s+]

one over the eight [1920s+] (orig. UK milit.:
   referring to the 'acceptable' consumption of
   eight pints of beer)

plastered [1910s+] (lit. 'bombed')

stonkered [1920s+] (orig. Aus.; lit. 'put out of
   action')

●●●●●●●●●●●●●●●●●●●●●●●●●●●●●●●●●●●●

globular [20C]

golded [1970s+]

gone [1920s+]

gonzo [1970s+] (US)

goofed up [1950s+] (US)

goofy(-ass) [1920s+]

gravelled [mid-19C]

groatable [early 18C] (US)

gronked [1960s+] (US)

guzzled [1930s] (US)

H

hand and fist [20C] (rhy. sl. 'pissed')

hanging [20C] (Irish)

hard-up [1950s+]

hiccius (doccius) [18C]

hicksius doxius/hictius-doctius [18C]

hockey/hocky [late 18C–19C]

hocus [early 18C–early 19C]

hocus-pocus [18C]

honkers [1950s+]

hoodman [19C]

hooted [late 19C–1930s] (US)

hot [18C+] (US)

hot-headed [18C]

humpty-doo [1930s+] (Aus.)

half-a-brewer [late 19C]

half-cut [20C]

half-gone [19C]

half-half-and-half [late 19C]

I

in a bad way [20C]

in for [1910s–20s]

in la-la land [1980s+] (US)

in one's ale(s) [late 16C–early 17C]

in one's armour [17C–early 19C]

in one's beer [late 17C–18C]

in one's cups [early 18C+]

in one's pots [early 17C]

in the bag [1940s] (orig. US; *bag* = a pot of beer)

in the gun [mid-17C–late 18C]

in the tank [20C]

in the wrapper [1940s] (orig. US)

incog [19C]

inked [late 19C+] (Aus./N.Z.)

inky(-poo) [1900s–60s] (Aus.)

ishkimkisk [18C–late 19C] (Shelta)

○○○○○○○○○○○○○○○○○○○○○○○○○○○○○○○○
Illuminated

bit lit [1920s+]

bright in the eye [late 19C–1920s]

illuminated [1920s+]

lit to the gills [20C]

lit (up) [1910s+]

lit up like a Christmas tree [20C] (very drunk)

lit up like Broadway [20C] (very drunk)

lit up like Main Street [20C] (very drunk)

lit up like Times Square [20C] (very drunk)

○○○○○○○○○○○○○○○○○○○○○○○○○○○○○○○○

lit up like a Christmas tree

J

jagged [1930s+]

jammed [1920s] (US)

jiggered [mid-19C+]

jingled [late 19C–1930s] (US)

john bull [1960s+] (Aus.; rhy. sl. 'full')

K

kalied/kaylied [1930s+] (from SE *alcohol*)

kanurd/kennurd [mid-19C] (backslang)

kaschnickered [1970s] (US Black)

kenird [late 19C] (backslang)

L

laid to the bone [1960s–70s] (US Black)

langered/langers [20C] (Irish)

leery [early 18C+] (US)

letting the finger ride the thumb [18C]

loaded (down) [late 19C+] (orig. US)

loaded to the earlobes [late 19C+]

loaded to the gills [late 19C+]

loaded to the muzzle [late 19C+]

loaded to the tailgate [late 19C+]

locked [20C] (Irish)

locussed [mid–late 19C]

Muzzy and moony:
confusion-related terms from M to W

mixed [mid–late 19C]

moony/mooney [20C]

muddled [late 17C+]

muggy [mid-19C]

muzzy [mid-18C+]

noddy headed [mid-19C–1900s]

non compos [late 19C+]

not all there/not quite there [mid-19C+]

numb [1910s–50s] (US)

obfuscated [mid-19C]

oddish [late 19C–1900s]

off one's nut [mid-19C+]

speechless [late 19C]

stunned [1910s–30s] (Aus./N.Z.)

stupid [1980s+]

tangled [late 19C–1900s] (Aus.)

woozled [1900s–20s]

○○○○○○○○○○○○○○○○○○○○○○○○○○○○○○○○○○○

looped [1970s+] (US)

loop-legged [1940s+] (US)

loopy [1920s+]

M

making Ms and Ts [late 18C–mid-19C] (punning on *MT*, i.e. 'empty')

martin drunk [19C] (*St Martin's evil* = drunkenness)

mickey finished [1950s] (US)

mizzled [late 16C–late 19C]

moccasined [mid-19C] (US)

mokus [1950s–70s] (US: drunk but wanting another drink)

molly [1960s–70s] (Aus.)

molo/molared/molled/mowlow [20C] (Aus.)

mopped up [18C+]

moppy [early 19C–1940s]

mops and brooms/all mops and brooms [19C+]

mortal [mid-18C–mid-19C]

motto [1920s] (tramp)

N

nazie/nazey [late 17C–mid-19C]

nazzy [mid-19C]

nicely, thank you [1920s–50s]

O

off one's bean [20C]

off one's face [1960s+]

°°°°°°°°°°°°°°°°°°°°°°°°°°°°°°°°°°°°°

Malted and mashed:
drink-related terms from M to P

malted [19C]

malty [early–mid-19C]

mashed [1940s+] (US; from the brewer's *mash*)

mulled (up) [1920s–70s]

oiled (up) [mid-18C+] (orig. US)

on the grog [1950s+]

on the juice [1950s+]

pickled [mid-17C+]

podgy [18C–mid-19C] (?from Italian *poco acqua*, a little water)

poggled [20C] (*poggle* = rum)

pogy [late 18C–early 19C]

pruned [19C] (*prune-juice* = hard liquor)

°°°°°°°°°°°°°°°°°°°°°°°°°°°°°°°°°°°°°

off one's gourd [1960s+]

on a bat [mid-19C+] (orig. US)

on sentry [late 19C–1910s]

out of control [1980s+] (US)

out of shape [1970s+] (US)

overtaken [early 18C–mid-19C]

over the line [1920s]

P

paid [mid-17C]

pepst [16C]

perked [late 19C] (Aus./N.Z.)

pervin' [1990s] (US Black teen)

piffed/piffled [20C] (US)

pifflicated [1900s–30s]

pinko [1920s–40s] (Aus.)

piped [1910s–50s] (US)

pissed(-up) [20C]

plonked-up [1910s+] (Aus.)

plootered [1920s+] (Scot.)

plotzed [20C]

ploughed/plowed [mid-19C+]

poddy [1900s–10s]

poegaai/poeg-eyed [1940s+] (S. Afr.; Dutch *pooien*, to tipple)

polled off [20C]

pot-shaken [17C]

potsick [19C]

Q

queer in the attic [19C]

quick tempered [19C]

R

raddled [late 17C]

rammaged [18C]

rat-arsed [1980s+]

ratted [1980s+] (UK society)

rattled [late 19C+]

○○○○○○○○○○○○○○○○○○○○○○○○○○○○○○○○
Salted and swilled:
drink-related terms from R to W

rum bag [20C]

salted [18C]

sap-happy [20C] (US; *sap* = juice)

shaved [19C] (*shave* = a drink)

slopped [1920s+]

stung [1910s+] (Aus.; *stingo*, a type of strong ale)

swiggled [19C]

swilled [16C]

swipey [late 18C–late 19C] (*swipes*, a type of thin beer)

swizzled [mid-19C+] (*swizzle* = intoxicating liquor)

swozzled [mid-19C+]

tubed [1960s+] (Aus. sl. *tube*, a can of beer)

well-oiled [20C] (*neck oil* = drink)

winey [mid-19C]

○○○○○○○○○○○○○○○○○○○○○○○○○○○○○○○○

ratty [mid-19C+] (US)

rileyed [late 19C] (US)

ripe [early 19C–1920s]

rocky [1920s+]

roostered [mid-19C–1900s] (US)

rosin-drunk [20C]

rotto [1920s] (Irish)

ruined/ruint [1960s+] (orig. US Black)

S

salt junk [late 19C–1900s] (rhy. sl. 'drunk')

salted [18C]

Salvation Army [late 19C] (rhy. sl. 'barmy')

schizzed [1950s+]

scooped [19C]

scratched [early 17C]

scraunched/scronched [20C] (US)

screwed [mid-19C+]

screwy [19C]

scrooched [1920s] (US)

seeing double [19C]

sheet in the wind [mid-19C+]

sherberty [late 19C]

shicker/shick/shiker/shikker [late 19C+] (mainly Aus./N.Z.; Hebrew *shikor*, drunk)

○○○

Maxed and mellow:
positively drunk terms from H to T

happy [18C+]

having a buzz on [mid-19C+] (orig. US; mildly intoxicated)

having an edge on [late 19C–1960s] (mildly intoxicated)

heady [late 17C–early 18C]

hearty [mid-19C–1910s]

in good fettle/in proper fettle [late 19C–1910s]

inspired [late 19C+]

jolly [19C] (mildly drunk)

looking lively [mid-19C+]

maxed [19C+]

maxed out [1970s+]

mellow [late 17C–18C]

miraculous [19C] (Scot.)

primed [1950s+]

quite the gay drunkard [late 19C] (mildly intoxicated)

salubrious [19C]

snug [19C]

spiffed [mid-19C] (orig. Scot.)

spreeish [19C]

stoked (up)/stoked on [1960s+] (orig. Aus.)

teed up [1920s+]

○○○

shickery [late 19C–1900s]

ship-wrecked [late 19C–1900s]

skimished/skimmished [20C] (usu. tramp)

snootered/snooted [19C+]

snopsy [19C] (US)

snozzled [1930s+] (US)

so [late 19C–1950s]

so-so [mid–late 19C]

sprung [19C]

squiffed [late 19C+]

starchy [mid-19C+]

steamboats [1980s+]

steamed up [1920s+]

steaming [20C]

stewed (up) [mid-18C+]

stitched [1920s+]

stoned (out) [1940s+]

subtle [17C]

T

talking to Jamie Moore [late 19C–1900s] (Scot.)

tall [1930s–40s] (US Black)

there [1930s] (US)

through [1990s] (US Black/teen)

tight [early 19C+]

tin hat [late 19C]

tipped [early 18C]

Tipperary [late 18C]

tipply [1910s–30s]

tired [1960s+]

tishy [1910s–30s]

tonic [late 19C+] (Aus.)

top-heavy [mid-17C–mid-19C]

○○○○○○○○○○○○○○○○○○○○○○○○○○○○○○
Tanky and tinned: receptacle-related terms

bottled [1920s–40s]

boxed [1930s+] (US)

canned (up) [1910s–40s]

corked [late 19C+]

corky [17C–19C]

jarred [1940s+]

jugged [1920s–70s] (US)

potted/poted [1920s+] (US)

smelling of the cork [19C]

tanked (up) [late 19C+]

tanky [1930s+] (US)

tinned [1940s+]

○○○○○○○○○○○○○○○○○○○○○○○○○○○○○○

corked

topped up [1960s+]

toppy [late 19C–1910s]

torrid [late 18C–mid-19C]

totalled (out) [1970s+] (orig. US)

tow row [late 18C–early 19C]

toxed/toxt [mid-17C]

trolleyed [1990s]

trousered [1990s]

tuned (up) [1920s+] (US)

U

umpty-doo [1910s+] (Aus.)

under [1940s+]

under the influence [late 19C+] (orig. US)

under the weather [mid-19C+]

unpaved [late 19C]

up in one's hat [19C]

up one's sleeve [late 19C]

up the pole [late 19C+]

V

vrot [1990s] (S. Afr.; Dutch *verotten*, to rot)

W

wall-eyed [1920s–30s] (US)

weary [early 18C–1900s]

well away [1920s+]

well to live [17C]

well under [1910s+] (Aus.)

wellied [1990s+]

well-loaded [late 19C+] (orig. US)

well-sprung [1910s–30s]

what-nosed [19C]

whiffled [1930s]

whistled [1930s+] (orig. milit.)

wired (up) [1960s+]

wollied [1980s]

worse for wear [20C]

wrapt up in warm flannel [late 18C–early 19C]

wrong all round the corner [late 19C–1920s]

Y

yaupy/yaupish [19C]

Z

zigzagged/zigzag [1910s+]

zippered [1980s+]

LEAKY AND LATHERED: WETNESS-RELATED TERMS

all wet [early 18C+]

awash [20C]

bladdered [1980s+]

buoyant [20C]

creamed [1960s+] (US; very drunk)

damp [early 19C] (US)

drenched [1920s–60s] (US; very drunk)

gargled [mid-19C+]

glued [1940s–60s] (US)

greased [1920s–50s] (US)

lathered [1910s–40s] (orig. Aus.)

leaky [late 19C]

lubricated [1920s+] (orig. US)

melted [20C]

moist round the edges [1900s–20s]

newted [1970s+]

on the ooze [1920s+]

saturated [late 19C–1930s+] (very drunk)

sauced [1940s+] (orig. US)

sauced up [1940s+] (US)

sloshed [late 19C+]

soaked [mid-18C+]

sodden [1930s]

soppy [1910s+]

soused (up) [17C+]

sozzled/sossled [late 19C+] (dial. *sossle*, a liquid mess)

waterlogged [1910s–20s] (very drunk)

wazzocked [1980s+] (dial. *wass*, to urinate)

wet [early 18C–mid-19C]

LAME AND LEGLESS: UNSTEADINESS-RELATED TERMS

crooked [mid-18C+]

lame [1950s+]

legless [1970s+]

rolling [20C]

○○○

Decks-awash:
naval and maritime terms

decks-awash [late 19C+]

getting the yellow fever [19C] (from the *yellow* parti-
coloured coat worn by inmate sailors at the Greenwich
Naval Hospital who were caught drunk)

half seas over [late 17C+] (a boat that has shipped
water is unstable)

half the bay over [late 19C]

listing to starboard [19C+]

loaded to the gunnels [late 19C+]

loaded to the Plimsoll Mark [late 19C+] (from the
plimsoll line which marks the limit of loading a ship)

needing a reef taken in [19C] (orig. naut.)

three sheets to the wind/three sheets over
[mid-19C+] (i.e. unstable: a ship carrying three sails to
the wind is top-heavy)

overseas [1930s]

oversparred [19C]

over the bay [late 18C–late 19C] (US)

over the line [1920s]

over the plimsoll [1920s+] (N.Z.)

shaking a cloth in the wind [late 18C–mid-19C]

too many cloths in the wind [late 19C]

○○○

skew-whiff [mid-18C+]

slewed [mid-19C+]

squiffy [1940s+]

swinny [19C]

swively [late 19C–20C]

tangle-footed [mid–late 19C]

tangle-legged [late 19C]

topsy boozy [late 19C]

topsy frizy [late 18C–late 19C]

tossed/tost [19C]

tostificated [19C]

tweaked/tweeked [1980s+] (US campus)

○○○○○○○○○○○○○○○○○○○○○○○○○○○○○○○
Under the table

belly up [1920s+]

below the mahogany [20C] (*mahogany* = the bar, beneath which the drinker has slipped)

lapping the gutter [19C]

low in the saddle [20C] (orig. US)

stretched [20C] (very drunk; i.e. *stretched* out on the floor)

under the table [mid-19C+]

watching the ant races [1970s+]

○○○○○○○○○○○○○○○○○○○○○○○○○○○○○○○

BASTED AND BATTERED: VIOLENCE-RELATED TERMS

basted [20C]

battered [late 19C+]

belted [1930s+] (US)

biffed [1920s] (US)

bitten by a barn-mouse [late 18C–early 19C]

bitten by the tavern bitch [17C–18C]

blasted [1970s+] (very drunk)

blitzed [1960s+] (very drunk)

blown up [1970s+] (US)

boiled [1920s+]

bombed [1950s+] (orig. US)

brained [1990s+]

buckled [1980s+] (Irish)

caned [1980s+] (very drunk)

clobbered [1940s+]

conked [1950s] (US)

crocked [1920s+]

crocko [1920s+]

cut [18C+]

cut over the head [18C]

dagged [mid-17C–18C]

damaged [mid-19C+] (orig. US)

hit on the head by the tavern bitch

done over [19C+]

electrified [20C]

floored [early 19C]

fractured [20C] (very drunk)

fried [1920s+] (very drunk)

hammered [1950s+] (very drunk)

hit on the head by the tavern bitch [17C–18C]

hit under the wing [mid-19C]

jug-bitten [early 17C]

lashed [1990s+]

nailed up [mid-19C] (US)

scammered [mid-19C]

shattered [1930s+]

shellacked [1920s–40s] (US; lit. 'varnished')

shredded [1980s+] (US teen)

slugged [20C] (US)

smashed [1940s+] (very drunk)

snockered/schnockered [1970s+] (?dial. *snock*, a blow)

○○○○○○○○○○○○○○○○○○○○○○○○○○○○○○○
Polluted and putrid

afflicted [early 18C+]

corroded [1970s+] (very drunk)

flawed [19C]

knocked up [mid 19C+]

lumpy [early–mid-19C] (mildly drunk)

palatic/parlatic [late 19C+] (*paralytic*)

paralysed [1950s+]

petrified [20C] (very drunk)

polluted [1910s+] (very drunk)

putrid [20C]

reeking [20C]

rotten [20C] (Aus.)

sewed up [mid-19C]

stinking [1910s] (very drunk)

○○○○○○○○○○○○○○○○○○○○○○○○○○○○○○○

●●●●●●●●●●●●●●●●●●●●●●●●●●●●●●●●●●●●●●●
Shot

cupshot [late 16C–late 18C]

grapeshot [19C]

half-shot [mid-19C+] (orig. US)

overshot [early 17C+]

pot-shot [early 17C–mid-19C]

shot [mid-19C+] (US/Aus./N.Z.)

shot full of holes [1910s+] (Aus./N.Z.)

shot in the neck [early–mid-19C] (US)

●●●●●●●●●●●●●●●●●●●●●●●●●●●●●●●●●●●●●●●

smiflicated/smifligated [20C] (orig. US)

spiflicated [20C] (orig. US; lit. 'thrashed')

squashed [1970s+] (very drunk)

swacked [1940s+] (very drunk; dial. *swack*, a blow)

swacko [1940s+] (very drunk)

swattled [19C] (*swaddle*, to beat up)

thrashed [1980s+] (US)

thumped over the head with Samson's jawbone [19C] (the biblical *Samson* was supposedly drunk when he was stripped of his hair-engendered powers)

trashed (out) [1970s+] (very drunk)

twisted [1950s+] (orig. US; very drunk)

○○○○○○○○○○○○○○○○○○○○○○○○○○○○○○○○○○○
Dead

croaked [20C]

dead [19C]

deado/deadoh [late 19C–1910s]

dead to the (wide) world/out to the wide [late 19C+]

down among the dead men [mid-19C]

embalmed [20C]

laid out [1920s+] (US)

rigid [1960s+] (very drunk)

stiff [mid-18C+] (orig. US; very drunk)

wasted [1960s+] (very drunk)

wasto [1990s] (utterly overcome by drink)

○○○○○○○○○○○○○○○○○○○○○○○○○○○○○○○○○○○

OUT OF ONE'S GOURD: DRUNK ON CAMPUS

annihilated [1970s+] (orig. US campus: very drunk)

baked [late 18C–1900s] (US campus)

bashed [1980s] (US campus)

blitzkrieged [1970s+] (US campus; very drunk)

blown (out) [1970s+] (US campus)

blue-eyed [mid-19C] (US campus)

bobo [1980s+] (US Black/campus)

boohonged [1980s+] (US campus)

caked [1990s] (US campus)

choked [1990s] (US campus)

comatose [1980s+] (US campus)

comboozelated [1970s+] (US campus)

commode-hugging drunk [1970s+] (US campus; very drunk)

fogmatic [mid-19C] (US campus)

golfed [1990s+] (US campus)

heated [1980s+] (US campus)

hiddy [1980s+] (US campus)

invertebrated [1980s+] (US campus)

loose [1960s+] (US campus)

commode-hugging drunk

Acronymic

f.u.b.a.r. [1940s+] (US campus; very drunk; *fucked up beyond all recognition*)

k.o.'ed [1960s–70s] (US; *knocked out*)

o.o.c. [1980s+] (US campus; *out of control*)

o.t.t. [1980s+] (very drunk indeed; *over the top*)

○○○○○○○○○○○○○○○○○○○○○○○○○○○○○○○○○○○

mindfucked [1980s+] (US campus)

nailed [1980s+] (US campus)

otis [1980s+] (US campus)

paved [1990s] (US campus)

ramped [1990s] (US campus)

ranked [1990s] (US campus)

ripped out of one's gourd [1980s+] (US campus)

ripskated [1990s] (US campus)

rocked [1980s+] (US campus)

smuckered [1970s] (US campus)

tattered [1980s+] (US campus)

ted [1980s+] (US campus; *wasted*)

toe (up)/torn up [1990s] (US Black/campus)

tore out of the frame [1970s] (US campus)

tore up [1950s+] (US Black/campus)

torqued [1980s+] (US campus)

vegetable [1970s] (US campus; very drunk)

whazood [1970s+] (US campus)

whipped/whooped/whupped [1980s] (US campus)

zoolooed [1970s] (US campus)

○○○○○○○○○○○○○○○○○○○○○○○○○○○○○○○○○○○
On the skite:
engaged in serious drinking

on a brannigan [late 19C+] (US)

on a skate [20C]

on a tipple [late 18C+]

on the floor [20C]

on the fritz [20C]

on the go [early 19C]

on the mop [19C+]

on the muddle [20C]

on the ramble [20C]

on the ran-tan [early 18C–mid-19C]

on the rap [late 19C]

on the reraw/on the ree-raw [mid-19C]

on the scoop/on the scoot [1900s–10s] (Aus.)

on the shicker [late 19C+] (mainly Aus./N.Z.;
    Hebrew *shikor*, drunk)

on the skite [20C] (Irish)

on the tiddley [mid-19C+]

○○○○○○○○○○○○○○○○○○○○○○○○○○○○○○○○○○○

VERY VERY DRUNK INDEED

arseholed/assholed [20C]

ballocked [1980s+]

blighted/blighting [1910s–40s]

blind [early 17C+] (orig. Und.)

blind as Chloe [early 19C+]

blinko [1950s] (US)

blithered [1910s+] (Aus.)

block-and-block [early–mid-18C] (US)

blotto [1910s+]

bullet-proof [1920s+] (orig. US Black)

bungs up [20C] (US)

bushwhacked [1960s] (orig. US)

buttwhipped [1990s+]

cacko [1960s] (Aus.)

clear [late 17C–late 18C]

cunted [1990s]

cut in the back [mid-17C–mid-19C]

cut in the leg [late 17C–late 18C]

dog-drunk [early 17C; mid-19C+]

done up [late 18C–early 19C]

doodle-ally/doodlally [1940s–50s]

doolally [late 19C+]

drunkin/drunking [1950s+] (W.I.)

faced [1980s+] (US teen; shit*faced*)

fighting drunk/fighting tight [20C]

fuckfaced [1940s+]

gonzoed [1970s+] (US)

guttered [1990s+]

hog-drunk [1950s–60s] (US)

hog-whimpering [20C] (US)

honking [1940s+]

hoodman blind [19C]

in one's royal [20C] (W.I.)

in the ditch [1980s+] (US)

in the jigs [1970s+]

mauled [late 17C–mid-19C]

○○○○○○○○○○○○○○○○○○○○○○○○○○○○○○○

Stewed and tight

stewed as a prune [1920s+]

stewed to the gills [1920s+]

stewed to the ears [1920s+]

stewed to the eyeballs [1920s+]

tight as a boiled owl/tight as an owl
[late 19C+] (US)

tight as a drum [20C]

tight as a fart [20C]

○○○○○○○○○○○○○○○○○○○○○○○○○○○○○○○○○

◦◦◦◦◦◦◦◦◦◦◦◦◦◦◦◦◦◦◦◦◦◦◦◦◦◦◦◦◦◦◦◦◦◦◦◦◦
'Full as a bitch'

bitch fou [17C+] (Scot.; lit. 'full as a bitch')

fou [late 17C+] (Scot. pron. of 'full')

greetin' fou [17C+] (Scot. *greet*, to cry)

piper fou [late 18C–19C]

pissing fou [19C]

roaring fou [19C]

◦◦◦◦◦◦◦◦◦◦◦◦◦◦◦◦◦◦◦◦◦◦◦◦◦◦◦◦◦◦◦◦◦◦◦◦◦

mortallious [19C]

mouldy [mid-19C]

nigger drunk [1940s–60s] (US)

out of one's kug [1960s] (US)

out of one's tits/off one's tits [1970s+]

out to it [1940s+] (Aus.)

over the top [1980s+]

owl-eyed/owly-eyed [1900s–60s] (US)

paralytic [1910s+] (orig. Aus.)

pissed to the ears [1950s+]

pissed up [1910s+]

pissy-arsed [20C]

pissy-drunk [20C] (US)

pixillated/pixilated/pixolated [1930s+]

shitface [1960s+] (orig. US)

shit-faced/shite-faced [1960s+] (orig. US)

soupy [late 19C]

stinko [1920s+]

stony blind [1920s–30s] (Aus.)

stoving [20C] (Ulster)

translated [late 19C] (UK society)

two tin hats, three tin hats [late 19C]

whistled drunk [mid-18C]

wiped out [1940s+]

wrecked [1960s+]

DRUNK AS ...

drunk as a bastard [late 18C]

drunk as a bat [late 18C]

drunk as a beggar [late 18C]

drunk as a besom [late 18C]

drunk as a brewer's fart [late 18C]

drunk as a cook [late 18C]

drunk as a coon [late 18C]

drunk as a cootie [20C]

drunk as a dog [late 18C]

drunk as a duck (and don't give a fuck/quack)
    [1910s+]

drunk as a fiddler [late 18C]

○○○○○○○○○○○○○○○○○○○○○○○○○○○○○○○○○○

Iced to the eyebrows:
phrases for extreme drunkenness

banged up to the eyes [mid-19C–1920s]

bent out of shape [1960s+]

blue-blind paralytic [1910s] (Aus.)

drunk to the pulp [1970s] (US Black)

fried (to the gills) [1920s+]

fried to the tonsils [1920s+]

full to the bow-tie [1950s]

full to the bung [mid–late 19C]

full to the gills [1910s+] (orig. US)

in a terrible state of chassis [1920s+] (Irish)

knee-walking drunk [1970s+] (US)

so drunk that he opened his shirt collar to piss [19C]

tanked to the wide [late 19C+]

tired and emotional [1960s+]

too numerous to mention [late 19C]

unable to hit the ground with one's hat [20C] (US)

whittled as a penguin [1960s] (Aus.)

○○○○○○○○○○○○○○○○○○○○○○○○○○○○○○○○○○○○

drunk as a fiddler's bitch [late 18C]

drunk as a fish [late 18C]

drunk as a fly [late 18C]

drunk as a fowl [late 18C]

drunk as a (fresh-)boiled owl [late 19C+]
(orig. US)

drunk as a Gosport fiddler [late 18C]

drunk as a hog [late 18C]

drunk as a king [late 18C]

drunk as a little red wagon [late 18C]

drunk as a log [late 18C]

drunk as a lord [late 18C]

drunk as a monkey [late 18C]

drunk as an emperor [late 18C]

drunk as a Perraner [late 18C]

drunk as a pig [late 18C]

drunk as a piper [late 18C]

drunk as a pissant [1930s+] (Aus.)

drunk as a poet [late 18C]

drunk as a polony [late 19C]

drunk as a rat [19C+]

drunk as a rolling fart [late 18C]

drunk as a skunk in a trunk [late 18C]

drunk as a sow [late 18C]

drunk as a swine [late 18C]

Full as ...

full as a boot [1950s] (Aus.)

full as a bull [1950s+]

full as a bull's bum [1960s+] (Aus.)

full as a fairy's phone book [1960s+] (Aus.)

full as a fiddler/full as a fiddler's fart [1960s+]

full as a goat [late 19C+]

full as a goog [1940s+] (Aus.; *goog* = egg)

full as a goose [1940s+] (Aus.)

full as a lord [1940s+] (Aus.)

full as an egg [1960s] (Aus.)

full as a seaside shithouse on Boxing Day
[1960s+] (Aus.: in Australia Christmas falls in
mid-summer)

full as a state school (hat rack) [1960s+] (Aus.)

full as a tick [1920s+]

full as a tun [18C]

full as the Bourke Street tram [1960s+] (Aus.)

full as the family po [1960s+] (Aus.)

full as two race trains [1980s] (Aus.)

○○○○○○○○○○○○○○○○○○○○○○○○○○○○○○○○○○

○○○○○○○○○○○○○○○○○○○○○○○○○○○○○○○○○
Pissed as ...

pissed as a chook [1960s+] (N.Z.)

pissed as a fart [20C]

pissed as a newt [20C]

pissed as a parrot [1990s] (Aus.)

pissed as a rat [20C]

pissed as arseholes [1960s+]

○○○○○○○○○○○○○○○○○○○○○○○○○○○○○○○○○

pissed as a newt

D.P.

drunk as a tapster [late 18C]

drunk as a wheelbarrow [late 18C]

drunk as Chloe [early 19C+]

drunk as cooter brown [1900s–40s] (orig. US Black)

drunk as David's sow/drunk as Davy's sow
  [late 17C+]

drunk as dogshit [1980s+]

drunk as floey [late 19C–1900s]

BEING AND GETTING DRUNK

TO BE DRUNK

be a passenger on the Cape Ann stage [mid-19C] (US
  campus)

bet one's kettle [20C] (to be so drunk that one bets one's
  valued possessions)

burn one's shoulder [20C]

carry a turkey on one's back [19C]

clip the King's English [late 17C–late 18C] (to slur one's
  words when drunk)

come from Liquorpond Street [early 19C–1900s]

crash a bottle [16C]

dip one's bill/dip the bill [17C] (to be mildly drunk)

drive the brewer's horse [19C]

feel funny [early 19C+]

float [1950s+]

fly [1950s+]

hang one on [1940s+]

have a bag on [1940s+] (US)

have a bit on [mid-19C]

have a cab [late 19C]

have a cup too much [mid-17C–19C]

have a few (too many) [20C] (orig. Aus.)

have a glow on [1940s+] (orig. US)

have a heat on [1910s–30s]

have a hummer going [1960s+] (US; *hummer* = a heavy drinking session)

have a pot in the pate [mid-17C–mid-18C]

have a sniff of the barmaid's apron [1920s+]

have a snootful [1910s+] (US)

have a tip on [1900s–20s]

have a white coat [late 19C]

have ballast on board [late 19C+]

have been in the sun [mid-18C]

have been standing too long [mid-19C]

have bread and cheese in one's head [mid-17C–mid-18C]

have business of both sides of the way [18C]

have caught a fox [17C–19C]

have corns in the head [mid-18C–mid-19C]

have drink taken [1920s+]

have had enough [mid-18C+]

have had one or two [late 19C+]

have hot balls [1980s+] (US campus)

have malt above the water [19C]

have malt above the wheat [mid-16C]

have one too many [20C]

have one's barrel full [late 19C] (US)

have one's eyes opened [20C]

have one's little hat on [18C]

have one's nuff [late 19C–1910s] (orig. milit.)

have one's pots on [19C]

have one's sails high [1940s–50s] (US Black)

have seen the French king [17C]

have the sun in one's eyes [mid-19C]

look through a glass [19C]

lose one's legs [mid–late 18C]

lose one's rudder [20C]

shoe the goose [early 17C]

show drink [late 19C] (US)

show it [20C]

tie one on [1950s+]

wave a flag of defiance [late 19C–1910s]

wear the barley cap [late 16C–late 17C]

○○

To be extremely drunk

burn with a low blue flame [1960s+]

can't find one's arse (with both hands) [20C]

can't say 'British constitution' [late 19C]

can't say 'naval intelligencer' [20C]

can't see a hole in a forty-foot ladder [late 19C+]

catch a fox [late 17C–18C] (*fox* = to make drunk)

go to bed in one's boots [late 19C–1900s]

have a beer in [1900s] (N.Z.)

have a brick in one's hat [mid–late 19C] (orig. US)

have a load on [late 19C+]

have a skinful [late 18C+]

have more than one can carry [mid-18C+]

have breath strong enough to carry coal [late 19C] (orig. US)

have one's back teeth afloat [late 19C+]

have one's back teeth awash [1900s–10s]

have one's kidneys afloat [late 19C+]

knock out one's link [mid-18C]

play camels [late 19C] (Anglo-Ind.; from the *camel*'s large capacity for liquid)

smash hell through a gridiron [late 19C] (US)

walk on one's cap-badge [1910s+] (orig. milit.)

watch the ant races [1970s+]

○○

oooooooooooooooooooooooooooooooooo
To make drunk

disguise [mid-16C–mid-19C] (to make drunk)

fox [early 17C+]

fuzz [late 17C–early 18C]

oooooooooooooooooooooooooooooooooo

TO GET DRUNK

beer [late 18C+] (to get drunk on beer)

black up [1950s+] (W.I.; i.e. one becomes 'blind')

booze up [1960s]

bung one's eye [late 18C–19C] (i.e. to drink until one's eyes are 'bunged' or closed)

buy the sack [early 18C–early 19C] (*sack*, a type of white wine from Spain and the Canaries)

catch a face [late 19C+] (US)

catch the flavour/get the flavour [19C]

cop a buzz [1970s+] (US)

cop a reeler [1930s–50s] (US)

cop the brewery [mid-19C–1900s]

cork up [1960s] (US)

corn up [late 19C] (US)

fetch the brewer [mid-19C]

flip [1950s+]

get a jag on [late 17C+]

get a skinful/have a skinful [late 18C+]

get a snootful [1910s+]

get kailed up [1920s–30s]

get one's head bad/get one's head right [1960s–70s] (US Black)

get right [1950s+] (US Black)

get sloppy [1980s+] (US Black/campus)

get stoned [1950s+]

get stupid [1990s] (US Black/teen)

get a glow on [1940s+] (orig. US)

get one's nuff [late 19C–1910s] (orig. milit.)

go for veg [1970s] (US campus; i.e. one becomes a *vege*table)

go on the cousin sis [1920s+] (rhy. sl. *cousin sis* = the piss)

hit the bung [1930s]

hit the sauce [1940s+] (orig. US)

hunt a tavern fox [mid–late 17C]

hunt the fox [late 16C–17C]

iron [1950s] (Aus.)

kill one's dog [mid-18C] (the *dog* may be the 'black dog' of depression)

lush it around/lush it up [1950s+] (US)

lush up [late 19C+]

open a keg of nails [1930s] (US; to get drunk on corn whisky)

overheat one's flues [late 19C]

pepper 'em up [1970s+] (US Black)

pie out [1970s] (US campus; from *pie*-eyed)

poll off [late 19C]

powder one's hair [18C] (euph.)

prime oneself [19C]

put another nail in one's coffin [19C]

rock [20C]

shout oneself hoarse [late 19C–1900s]

slop up [late 19C–1920s]

souse [20C]

swallow a tavern token [late 17C–18C]

take in a cargo [early 19C]

throw on a face [late 19C+] (US)

tie a bag on [1940s+] (US)

tie on [1930s+] (US)

wash one's face in an ale clout [16C–17C]

wet one's neck [early 19C]

whip the cat [17C]

Travelling wildly

come home by rail [1930s+] (Aus.; i.e. one can only proceed by hanging on to things)

go Borneo [1970s+] (US campus; to get crazily drunk, from the presumed antics of the 'Wild Man of *Borneo*')

go for veg [1970s] (US campus; i.e. one becomes a *veg*etable)

go on the cousin sis [1920s+] (rhy. sl. 'go on the piss')

go to Jericho [late 18C–early 19C] (from *Jericho* as a place of exile)

go to Jerusalem [mid-18C–early 19C] (?drunkenness as the 'promised land')

go to Mexico [1950s+] (US; for US teenagers brief trips across the border to *Mexico* imply non-stop excess)

go to Putney (on a pig) [mid-19C]

row up Salt River [early 19C–1940s] (US)

see Indians [19C] (US)

see the lions [mid-19C+]

take a Burford bait [19C]

get one's nose painted

To get extremely drunk

bite one's grannam [17C]

burn one on [1950s+]

drown the shamrock [20C] (Irish; to
become very drunk on St Patrick's day)

fall in the thick [late 19C]

get one's nose painted [20C]

get one's shoes full [20C]

get one's soul in soak [19C]

get rats/have rats [mid-19C+]

get the gravel rash [mid-19C]

swallow a hare [late 17C–early 19C]

○○○○○○○○○○○○○○○○○○○○○○○○○○○○○○○○○○○○○

HANGOVERS

big head [late 19C]

brewer's asthma [1920s+] (Aus.; a very bad hangover)

carry-over [1940s]

cottonmouth [1960s+] (the dry mouth that comes
with a hangover)

fat-head [mid-19C+]

gallon distemper [early 19C–1900s]

head [late 19C+]

heebie-jeebies [1920s+]

hot coppers [19C] (a mouth and throat parched through excessive drinking)

jag [late 19C+]

jams [late 19C–1910s]

jim-jams [mid-19C–1950s] (orig US)

jitters [1920s+] (US)

katzenjammer [mid-19C+] (US; German *Katzen*, cats + *Jammer*, wailing)

long stale drunk [late 19C] (from the depression that follows the drinking bout)

miserables [late 19C–1920s]

morning after (the night before) [late 19C+]

noggin [19C+]

one [late 19C+]

quart mania [19C]

rats [mid–late 19C+]

thick head [20C]

HUNGOVER

chippy [late 19C]

crawsick [1920s+] (Irish)

cropsick [late 17C–18C] (feeling sick after a drinking bout)

fishy [mid-19C] (looking ill round the eyes after a drinking session)

fishy about the gills [late 19C]

hot-headed [18C]

hung [1940s+] (US)

mash-up [late 19C+]

oorie/oorey/oory [20C] (Ulster)

stale drunk [19C]

whipped [1940s] (US Black)

TO HAVE A HANGOVER

feel like a (fresh-)boiled owl [19C] (US)

feel like a stewed monkey [19C] (US)

have a head like a drover's dog [1940s+] (Aus.)

have a head on [mid-19C+]

have a mouth like a lorry driver's crotch [1960s+]

have a mouth like a nun's minge [1960s+]

have a mouth like the bottom of a cocky's cage
   [1960s+]

have a mouth like the bottom of a parrot's cage
   [1940s+]

have a mouth like the bottom of a birdcage
   [1920s+]

have a mouth like the inside of an Arab's armpit
   [1940s+]

**have a mouth like the inside of an Arab's under-
   pants** [1940s+]

have cobwebs in one's throat [19C]

suffer a recovery [late 19C]

wear one's head large [late 19C]

wear the barley cap [late 16C–late 17C]

DELIRIUM TREMENS

barrel fever [late 18C+]

bat [20C]

bottle-ache [mid-19C–1900s]

cast-iron horrors [20C] (Anglo-Irish)

clanks [1980s+] (US)

dib-dabs [1940s]

diddleums [1920s+] (Aus.)

dingbats [1910s+]

gallon distemper [early 19C–1900s]

hoo-jahs/hoo-hoohs [1930s+] (Aus./US)

hop-head [20C]

horries [1950s+] (S. Afr.)

horrors [mid-18C+]

jerks [late 19C] (US)

jims [late 19C–1920s] (Aus.)

joe blakes [1940s+] (Aus./N.Z.; rhy. sl. 'shakes')

joe morgans [1920s] (N.Z.)

jumps [late 19C–1940s] (orig. US)

rams [20C]

screaming abdabs [1930s+]

shakes [late 19C+]

stonewall horrors [20C] (Anglo-Irish)

trembles [19C]

triangles [mid-19C]

uglies [late 19C–1900s]

whiskyhead [1940s+] (US)

○○○○○○○○○○○○○○○○○○○○○○○○○○○○○○○
Fantasy creatures

blue devils [18C]

bull horrors [1950s] (US)

ducks and drakes [1960s] (Aus.: rhy. sl. 'shakes')

jag snakes [late 19C] (US)

pink elephants [1930s+]

pink spiders [19C]

rattlesnakes [20C]

snakes [late 19C]

○○○○○○○○○○○○○○○○○○○○○○○○○○○○○○○

THE ULTIMATE
FUNCTION

TO DIE

answer the last round-up [20C]

become a landowner [19C–1900s] (playing on *landed estate*, a cemetery)

bite [1960s+] (US)

bite the big one [1970s+]

bite the dust/chew dust [mid-19C+]

blow out [mid-19C+] (US)

bowl off [mid-19C]

buck out [1920s–30s] (US West)

bung out [1900s] (N.Z.)

buy it [1920s+]

buy the farm [1940s+] (orig. US; referring to the wish of US military aviators to retire from combat, settle down and *buy a farm*)

buzz (off) [20C]

camp [mid-19C+] (Aus.)

cark (it)/kark [1970s] (Aus.)

cave [mid-19C+] (mainly US)

cease [1920s–50s] (US Black)

chalk out [late 19C]

check in [20C] (US)

check out [1950s+] (orig. US)

chuck (a) seven [late 19C+] (Aus.)

cock (up) one's toes [mid-19C]

come down in a pile [20C] (US)

come to a sticky end [1910s+]

conk [early 19C+] (US)

conk off [1940s] (orig. US)

cool [1930s+] (US)

cool it [1950s+] (US)

cop it (hot) [late 19C+]

cop off [late 19C] (US)

corpse [late 19C]

crap out [20C] (orig. US)

croak [early 19C+]

cut out [late 19C+] (US)

do a croak/pull a croak [1900s–20s] (US)

do a oner/do one's oner [1910s+] (Aus.)

○○○○○○○○○○○○○○○○○○○○○○○○○○○○○○○○
Join the angels

climb the golden staircase [late 19C] (US)

go aloft [late 18C+]

go trumpet-cleaning [late 19C] (the *trumpeter* in
  question being the angel Gabriel)

join the angels [19C]

join the great majority [20C]

play the harp [20C]

○○○○○○○○○○○○○○○○○○○○○○○○○○○○○○○○

ooooooooooooooooooooooooooooooooo
Journeys

go across the river [19C]

go home [late 19C]

go over the range [1930s–40s] (Aus.)

go to grass with one's teeth upward [19C]

go to shut-eye land [1940s] (W.I.)

go up Green River [mid–late 19C] (US; from the
name of a type of Texas-made knife)

go up Salt River [1940s] (US Black)

go west [late 16C+] (from the journey from
Newgate prison westward towards the gallows
at Tyburn)

leave town [1900s–50s] (US Black)

ooooooooooooooooooooooooooooooooo

drop [early 18C+]

drop off [20C]

drop off one's perch [18C+]

drop off the twig [20C]

drop one's leaf [19C]

drop out [20C]

eat it [1930s+]

fade out [1920s–50s] (orig. US)

finish one's circle [20C] (US: Western jargon. orig. used of a

dead cowman, whose jobs, when alive, included riding the
boundaries of the ranch)

finish one's row [20C] (US; the image is of a ploughman)

flake (out) [1930s+]

float [late 19C+] (Aus.)

fluke [20C]

fly the coop [mid-19C+] (US)

get the big one [1920s] (US)

get the gun [1900s] (US)

give the crow a pudding [late 16C–early 19C]

give the slip [19C]

go belly(-side) up [1920s+]

go conk [1920s+] (Aus.)

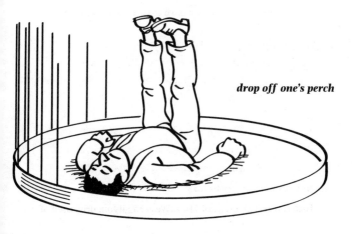

drop off one's perch

go for a Burton [1940s+] (orig. UK milit.)

go for six [1940s]

go off [mid–late 17C]

go off the hooks [mid-19C+]

go off the stocks [mid-19C+]

go out [1930s+] (Aus./US Black/prison)

go to glory [early 19C+]

go to grass [19C+] (US)

go to pot [19C+]

go to sleep [20C]

go to the pot [mid-19C]

go under [late 19C+] (orig. US)

●●●●●●●●●●●●●●●●●●●●●●●●●●●●●●●●●
Last suppers

go for one's tea [20C]

hand in one's dinner pail [1920s+]

kick the bucket/kick the can [16C+] (possibly
referring to the 16C manner of killing a pig,
whereby the animal was suspended from a beam
by the insertion of a piece of bent wood, known
as a *bucket*, behind the tendons of its hind legs;
as the pig dies it *kicks* out at the *bucket*)

lay down one's knife and fork [mid-19C+]

stick one's spoon in the wall [19C]

●●●●●●●●●●●●●●●●●●●●●●●●●●●●●●●●●

Resigned

call it a day [20C]

call it quits [20C]

turn one's face to the wall [1940s+]

○○○○○○○○○○○○○○○○○○○○○○○○○○○○○○○○○○○○○

hang up one's boots [mid-19C+]

hang up one's fiddle [mid-19C] (US)

hang up one's harness/hang up one's tackle [19C]

hang up one's hat [mid-19C+]

have one's number come up [20C]

hit the deep six [1960s+] (US)

hit the grit/hit the turf [19C+] (US)

hop off [late 18C]

hop the perch [late 19C+]

hop the twig [late 18C–early 19C] (UK Und.)

jack it [late 19C–1900s]

kick [early 18C+]

kickeraboo [mid-19C] (W.I.; i.e. '*kick the bu*cket')

kick in [20C] (US)

kick it [mid-19C+]

kick off [20C]

kick out [late 19C+]

kick up dust [19C]

**kick up one's heels/lay up one's heels/topple up one's
    heels/turn up one's heels** [late 16C+]

kiss off [1930s+] (US)

kiss the dust [20C] (orig. US)

knock off [mid-17C+]

knock over [late 19C–1900s]

k.o./kayo [20C] (US campus)

○○○○○○○○○○○○○○○○○○○○○○○○○○○○○○○○○
Maritime terms

answer the last muster [20C]

answer the last roll-call [20C]

coil one's ropes [20C] (US)

cut one's cable [19C]

cut the painter [mid-17C–mid-19C]

drop off the hook(s) [mid-19C–1920s]

give up the ship [19C]

go to Davy Jones's locker [mid-19C]

keel off/keel out [20C] (W.I.)

lose the number of one's mess [mid-19C]

sling one's hook [mid-19C]

slip one's breath [early 18C]

slip one's cable [late 18C]

slip one's wind [early–mid-19C]

○○○○○○○○○○○○○○○○○○○○○○○○○○○○○○○○○

lay 'em down [1930s–40s] (US)

lay up [late 19C] (US)

lay up in lavender [late 17C–18C]

leave the minority [late 19C]

muff [early 19C]

off [late 19C+]

pack in [1940s+]

pack up [1910s+] (orig. milit.)

pass out [late 19C]

pass the buck [19C+] (orig. US)

perch [late 19C]

peter out [mid-19C+]

pig out/pork out/pig it [mid-19C]

pike [mid-17C–1920s] (UK Und.)

pip off [1930s] [from the radio *pips* that signal a time-check]

pip (out) [1910s–20s]

poop out [1940s] (US Black)

pop off [18C+]

pop off the hooks [mid-18C+]

pop one's clogs [1970s+]

punch the clock [1920s+]

quit [1930s+] (orig. US)

quit it [1940s–50s] (US Black)

quit the scene [1950s] (US Black)

roll up [mid-19C+] (orig. US)

shoot one's star [late 19C–1900s]

shuffle off [1920s+] (from *Hamlet* III.i.67: 'When we have shuffel'd off this mortall coile')

skop [1960s+] (S. Afr.)

slam off [20C]

snuff (it) [mid-19C+]

split [late 18C–mid-19C]

sprout wings [20C] (US)

squiff it [1940s+] (Aus.)

step off [1920s]

step off the curb [20C] (US)

step out [mid-19C–1900s] (US)

stop ticking [1930s+]

◦◦◦◦◦◦◦◦◦◦◦◦◦◦◦◦◦◦◦◦◦◦◦◦◦◦◦◦◦◦◦◦
Sporting terms
drop the cue [20C]

go to the races [20C]

hang up one's harness [19C]

jump the last hurdle [19C]

peg out [19C]

strike out [20C] (US)

take the long count [19C]

throw in the sponge [19C]

◦◦◦◦◦◦◦◦◦◦◦◦◦◦◦◦◦◦◦◦◦◦◦◦◦◦◦◦◦◦◦◦

tail it [1920s+]   *jump the last hurdle*

take a blinder [mid-19C–1900s]

take a dirt nap [1990s] (US Black)

take gruel [late 19C]

take off [1930s+]

take the big jump [20C] (US)

take the count [late 19C–1900s]

take the last count/take the long count [1930s+] (US)

throw a seven [late 19C+] (Aus.)

throw in one's alley [1900s–10s] (Aus.)

throw sixes [20C]

tip [late 17C–early 18C]

○○○○○○○○○○○○○○○○○○○○○○○○○○○○○○○○○○○○○○
Cashing in

call off all bets [1930s–40s] (US Black)

cash in [late 19C+] (orig. US)

cash in one's checks [late 19C+] (orig. US)

cash in one's chips/throw in one's chips [late 19C+] (orig. US)

cash one's last check [20C]

cash out [1960s]

chuck one's hand in [late 19C+]

get one's checks [late 19C] (US)

hand in one's checks [mid-19C+] (US)

hand in one's chips [late 19C+]

pass in one's checks [mid-19C+] (orig. US)

pass in one's chips [late 19C+] (orig. US)

pass in one's marble(s) [1900s–50s] (Aus.)

pay one's last debt [1940s] (US Black)

put one's checks in the rack [1930s+] (US)

put one's cue in the rack [1980s+]

send in one's checks [mid-19C+] (US)

sign one's last check [20C] (US)

throw in one's cards [20C]

○○○○○○○○○○○○○○○○○○○○○○○○○○○○○○○○○○○○

tip off [late 17C–early 19C]

toss in one's agate [1900s] (Aus.; SE *agate*, a type of marble)

turn down one's cup [late 19C] (UK society)

turn one's toes up (to the daisies) [mid-19C+]

vrek [1910s+] (S. Afr.; Afrikaans, 'to die', usu. used of animals)

walk away [mid-19C]

DEATH

big blink [1970s–80s]

big jump [20C] (US)

big one [1930s] (US)

big sleep [1930s+] (orig. US)

cash-in [1920s] (US)

curtains [1910s+]

deep six [1920s–40s]

end of the ball-game [20C]

fade out [1920s–50s]

fall of the leaf [early 18C]

final curtain [20C]

finale [1940s] (US Black)

final thrill [1940s] (US Black)

great bounce [late 19C] (US)

happy hunting grounds [19C] (orig. US)

kiss off [1940s+]

k.o./kayo [1930s+] (orig. US; *knock out*)

kwy [late 19C] (Latin *quietus*, death)

last debt [1940s] (US Black)

last farewell [20C]

last goodbye [20C]

last muster [20C]

last out [1940s] (US Black)

last round-up [20C]

lights out [20C]

long goodbye [1950s+] (the title of a 1953 novel by Raymond Chandler)

old floorer [mid-19C–1920s]

○○○○○○○○○○○○○○○○○○○○○○○○○○○○○○○○○○○○○○
A whiff of the morgue
big chill [1980s+]

chill [1930s+]

cold storage [20C]

○○○○○○○○○○○○○○○○○○○○○○○○○○○○○○○○○○○○○○

○○○○○○○○○○○○○○○○○○○○○○○○○○○○○○○○○○○○○○
Death personified
great whipper-in [mid-19C–1920s]

Mr Grim/Old Mr Grim [late 18C; 1940s+]

old man Mose [1940s] (US Black; *Moses*)

○○○○○○○○○○○○○○○○○○○○○○○○○○○○○○○○○○○○○○

perch [early 18C]

pop-off [mid-19C] (US)

send-off [19C+]

terminal [1990s]

wind-up [19C+]

DEAD

all over [late 19C]

aloft [late 18C+]

assed-out [1980s+]

away [late 19C+]

backed [late 17C-early 19C]

belly up [1970s+]

bong [1940s+]

box city [1980s+] (US)

boxed [1960s+] (US)

busted [late 19C+]

cactus [1940s+] (Aus.)

cold [20C]

cold turkey [1930s–60s] (US)

conked [1920s+]

content [18C–early 19C]

croaked [20C]

dead-nuts [late 19C+] (US)

deado/deadoh [late 19C–1910s]

done for [late 19C+]

down for the last count/down for the long count [20C]

history [1970s+] (US)

hooked up [1920s]

in the flue [mid-19C]

in the grand secret [18C–19C]

kin teet [1950s] (W.I.: lit. 'skin teeth', from the drawing back
   of the skin from the teeth through rigor mortis)

knocked over [late 19C]

lying by the wall [15C–late 17C]

off the hooks [19C]

on ice [1920s+]

on the shelf [late 19C]

out [late 19C]

outed [20C] (orig. Aus.)

out of one's misery [early 19C+]

past it [mid-19C+]

pegged out [mid-19C+]

playing a harp [1920s+] (orig. US)

promoted [late 19C]

pushing clouds [1920s] (US)

put into one's cool crape [late 18C] (i.e. put into a shroud)

rubbed out [mid-19C]

scragged [mid-18C–19C]

playing a harp

shuffled out of the deck [20C]

slabbed and slid [1940s–50s] (UK prison)

slated [late 19C]

stiff [mid-18C+] (orig. US)

thrown for a loss [20C]

tits-up [1960s+] (orig. Can. prison)

toes up [mid-19C]

tucked away [20C] (Aus.)

○○○○○○○○○○○○○○○○○○○○○○○○○○○○○○○○○○○○
Gone west

gone [19C+] (US)

gone across/gone up [20C]

gone for the milk [20C] (Irish)

gone overboard [20C]

gone to pot [mid-19C+]

gone to Rotisbone/gone to Rot-His-Bone [late
  18C–early 19C] (punning on the religious
  colloquy of the Diet of *Ratisbon* and *rot-his-bone*)

gone west [late 16C+]

○○○○○○○○○○○○○○○○○○○○○○○○○○○○○○○○○○○○

○○○○○○○○○○○○○○○○○○○○○○○○○○○○○○○○○○○○
Dead in rhyming slang

brown bread [1990s]

buttered bread [20C]

currant bread [20C]

fried bread [20C]

gone to bed [20C]

loaf of bread [1930s]

potted head [20C]

toasted bread [20C]

wombat [20C] (Aus.; *'hors de combat'*)

○○○○○○○○○○○○○○○○○○○○○○○○○○○○○○○○○○○○

Six feet under

counting (the) worms [20C]

dirt-napping [1990s] (US Black)

grinning at the daisy roots [late 19C] (Anglo-Ind.)

potted (out) [mid-late 19C]

pushing up the daisies/licking up the daisies [20C]

put to bed with a mattock (and tucked up with a spade) [18C–early 19C]

put to bed with a pickaxe and shovel [19C]

six feet under [1930s+] (orig. US)

under the daisies [mid-19C+]

under the hatches [late 17C–19C]

under the sod [mid-19C+]

○○○

up the shoot [1950s]

up the spout [early 19C–1920s]

used up [mid-18C–mid-19C]

way of all flesh [late 19C]

THE CORPSE

bod [late 18C+]

buzzard bait [mid-19C+] (US: a corpse abandoned in the open)

buzzard meat [late 19C–1930s] (US)

Dead as …

dead as a dodo [20C]

dead as a doornail [mid-14C–late 16C]

dead as a hammer [mid-19C]

dead as a herring [mid-17C+]

dead as a maggot [1940s+] (Aus.)

dead as a tent-peg [19C–1910s]

dead as a wooden Indian [20C] (US)

dead as dogshit [1980s+]

dead as Hannah Emerson [19C+] (US)

dead as Hector [19C+] (US)

dead as Julius Caesar [late 19C–1900s]

dead as mutton [late 18C–1910s]

dead as small beer [19C]

∘∘∘∘∘∘∘∘∘∘∘∘∘∘∘∘∘∘∘∘∘∘∘∘∘∘∘∘∘∘∘∘∘∘∘∘∘∘∘

coffin meat [mid-19C] (US)

cold meat [late 18C+]

croaker [mid–late 19C]

croppy [1920s]

crow-bait [mid-19C+] (US; a corpse abandoned in the open)

dab [19C] (a drowned woman)

deader [mid–late 19C]

deadie [1970s]

dead meat [mid-19C+]

deado [1910s+]

dustman [late 18C]

floater [late 19C+] (orig. US; a corpse found *floating* in water)

flounder [19C] (a drowned man)

meat [late 16C+] (US)

pickles [19C] (a corpse brought in for dissection)

quarrom [mid-16C–mid-19C] (Italian *carogna*, a corpse)

rags and bones [1970s] (US Black; the corpse of a poor person)

seventeener [20C] (Aus.)

smear [20C] (Aus.: the corpse of a murdered person)

stiff [early 19C+]

stiff 'un [mid-19C+]

stiffy [late 19C–1900s]

tom noddy [20C] (US; rhy. sl. 'body')

wormbait [19C+]

○○○○○○○○○○○○○○○○○○○○○○○○○○○○○○○○○○
Cold comfort: sex with corpses
get some cold comfort [1980s+]

raid the ice box [1970s+]

slabbing [1970s+]

○○○○○○○○○○○○○○○○○○○○○○○○○○○○○○○○○○

THE HUMAN BODY:

A NORTH–SOUTH TOUR

THE HEAD

acorn [1900s] (US)

apple [20C]

attic [early 19C+] (orig. boxing)

barber's block [early 19C+]

bean [20C]

beezer [1910s+]

belfry [1900s–10s]

biscuit [19C]

block [mid-17C+]

boco [mid-19C+]

bonce [late 19C+]

brainbox [late 18C+]

brain bucket [mid-19C] (US)

brain-canister [mid–late 19C]

bundle of socks [late 19C+] (Aus.; rhy. sl. 'thinkbox')

cabeza [mid-19C+] (US, Southwest; Spanish)

calabash [mid-19C]

can [late 19C+]

canister [mid-19C]

casaba [1950s+] (US)

chump [19C+]

coco/cocoa/koko [early 19C+] (orig. US)

coconut [mid-19C+]

coke [1920s] (US)

cone [late 19C] (US)

conkhouse [20C] (US Black)

conkpiece [1940s] (US Black)

coop [1900s–20s] (US)

○○○○○○○○○○○○○○○○○○○○○○○○○○○○○○○○○○○
The head in rhyming slang

alive or dead [late 19C+]

ball of lead [1900s–10s]

crust of bread [20C]

Judge Dredd [1990s]

kelly ned [20C]

loaf (of bread) [1910s+]

lump of bread [1910s–20s]

lump of lead [mid-19C]

ned [1910s+] (orig. Aus.: 'kelly *ned*')

penn'orth of bread [20C]

pound [late 19C+] ('*pound* o' lead')

pound o' lead [late 19C–1900s]

ruby red [1900s]

twopenny [mid-19C–1930s] (*twopenny* loaf.
   i.e. 'loaf of bread')

Uncle Ned [1950s+]

○○○○○○○○○○○○○○○○○○○○○○○○○○○○○○○○○○○○○

oooooooooooooooooooooooooooooooooooo
Bald heads

billiard ball [19C]

cheesekop [1970s+] (S. Afr.; a shaven head)

chrome dome [20C]

fly rink [late 19C]

skating rink/flies' skating rink [1910s+]

oooooooooooooooooooooooooooooooooooo

costard [16C–late 18C]

coxcomb [late 16C–early 18C]

crock [1920s+] (US)

crown office [late 18C]

crudget [1920s+]

cruet [1940s+]

crumb [early–mid-19C] (US)

crumpet [19C–1920s]

cupola [late 19C–1950s] (US; Italian, 'dome')

deeache [mid-19C+] (backslang)

derby [1930s+]

ding-dong [1920s] (US)

dome [mid-19C+] (orig. US)

dome piece [1970s] (US)

doorknob [20C]

dop [1970s] (Dutch, 'shell')

dreambox [1910s–40s] (US Black)

egg [1920s–30s]

egghead [20C]

filbert [late 19C–1930s] (lit. 'hazelnut')

gable(-end) [late 19C]

garret [mid-19C+]

gourd [1970s+]

hat rack [18C; 1930s–60s]

head-piece [late 16C+]

intelligence department [1910s–20s]

jemmy [mid-19C]

jolly (nob) [late 18C–19C]

kabeezer [1960s]

knob [mid-17C; 1920s+]

knot [1950s–70s]

knowledge box [late 18C+]

kopgee/kop-jee [late 19C] (Dutch *kopje*, a small hill)

lemon [1920s–50s]

lid [late 19C+]

lob [18C]

lolly [mid-19C]

mazard [16C–19C] (SE *mazer*, a wood used to make drinking
  cups)

mellow roof [1930s–40s]

melon [1930s+]

moppery [early–mid-19C]

nana [1940s+]

nanny [late 18C] (UK Und.)

napper [late 17C–18C]

nob [late 17C+]

noddle [mid-16C+]

noggin [19C+]

noodle [19C+]

nuddikin [mid-19C]

nut [mid-19C+]

nutcracker [mid-19C–1950s]

nutter [1950s+]

onion [mid-19C+]

packy [1940s+] (lit. 'calabash fruit')

pannikin [late 19C–1930s] (Aus.)

penny-a-mile [late 19C–1920s] (rhy. sl. 'tile', lit. 'hat')

pimple [early 19C–1940s]

pipkin [mid-19C]

potato [20C]

poundrel [17C] (lit. 'scales')

pow [20C]

prune [1920s–50s]

pumpkin [19C]

pumpkin head [1970s]

roof [mid-19C–1940s]

roundem [mid-19C–1900s]

sconce [mid-16C–1950s]

scone [1940s+] (Aus./N.Z.)

swede [1920s+]

thinkbox [late 19C–1900s]

tibby [early 19C–1900s]

tombhead [1960s]

top deck [1920s+]

top end [late 19C]

top flat [late 19C]

top piece [mid-19C]

tuck [late 19C] (*tuck*-box, a
  container for food)

turnip [mid-19C+]

turnip-pate [late 17C–18C]

upper apartment [19C]

upper crust [early–mid-19C]

upper storey [late 18C–19C]

weathercock [late 19C]

wig [18C+]

wig-block [mid-19C–1920s]

prune

THE FACE

beauty mark/beauty spot [mid-19C] (US)

biscuit [19C]

black beezer [20C] (a black person's face)

button [19C+] (US)

chib [late 19C]

chiv [1910s] (Aus.)

chivy/chivvy [late 19C–1950s]

chump [19C+]

clock [mid-19C+]

counting-house [late 19C]

coupon [20C] (Scot.)

dial [early 19C+]

dial-plate/dial-piece [early–mid-19C]

eek [1950s+] (Polari)

esaff [late 19C] (backslang)

fatcha [20C] (Ling. Fr./Polari; Italian *faccia*, the face]

fiz [early 18C] (*phys*iognomy)

frontage [mid-19C+]

frontispiece [mid-19C]

geseech [late 19C–1900s] (Yiddish *gesicht*, the face)

grill [1980s+] (US Black/teen)

index [1930s–40s] (US Black)

jack-knife face [mid-19C+] (US)

kabeezer [1960s] (US; Spanish *cabeza*, the head)

kip [1990s+] (Scot.; lit. 'promontory')

kisser [mid-19C+] (orig. boxing)

kite [mid-16C–early 17C]

mag [late 19C]

map [late 19C+]

mazard/mazzard [16C–19C] (SE *mazer*, a wood used for making drinking cups)

○○○○○○○○○○○○○○○○○○○○○○○○○○○○○○○○
The face in rhyming slang

boat (race) [1940s+]

cherry ace [1940s–50s]

chevy chase [mid-19C–1950s]

chips and chase [1920s–40s] (US)

deuce and ace [late 19C+]

glass case [mid-19C]

handicap chase [20C]

jem mace [20C] (the name of a 19C prizefighter)

kipper (and plaice) [20C]

Martin Place [1930s+] (Aus.)

Peyton Place [1950s+] (US)

roach and dace [20C]

satin and lace [20C]

○○○○○○○○○○○○○○○○○○○○○○○○○○○○○○○○

○○○○○○○○○○○○○○○○○○○○○○○○○○○○○○○○○○○
Red and ugly faces

beetroot mug [late 19C–1910s] (a red face)

bracket-mug [19C] (an ugly face)

carbuncle face [late 17C–late 18C] (a face
  covered in boils and pimples)

grog blossom [18C+] (a red face caused by
  excessive, long-term drinking)

rogers [late 19C] (society; a ghastly face, from
  Samuel *Rogers*, a banker and poet with a notably
  aged countenance)

rum phiz/rum phyz [late 18C] (an odd-looking
  face)

splatter face [late 19C] (a broad face)

toddy blossom [19C] (a red face caused by
  excessive long-term drinking)

Tyburn collop [16C] (a miserable face)

ugly plug [19C] (an ugly face)

○○○○○○○○○○○○○○○○○○○○○○○○○○○○○○○○○○○

mizzard [early 17C–late 19C]

mug/mugg [18C+]

mums [late 18C–late 19C]

mun/mund/munn/munne [14C–late 19C]

muns/munns/munds [late 17C–mid-19C]

mush/moosh [mid-19C+] (orig. US)

muzzle [15C+]

neb [late 17C–early 19C]

nib [late 18C–mid-19C] (lit. 'beak')

pan [1910s+]

phiz/phyz/phyzog/fizzog/phizzog [late 17C+] (*physiog*nomy)

pisk [1930s]

plaque [1940s–60s] (Irish)

portrait [1900s] (US Black)

puss [late 19C+] (Irish *pus*, the mouth)

register [late 19C]

shif [1970s] (Aus.)

signboard [late 19C–1900s]

smiler [20C]

snout-piece [17C–19C]

title page [mid-19C]

upper rigging [late 19C–1900s] (US)

viz [1990s] (*vis*age)

whisker-bed [mid-19C]

THE EYES

beads (US)

blink [1900s–30s] (US)

blinker [18C–1950s; US mid-19C–20C]

blinkers [late 18C+]

blinks [mid-19C]

blues [1970s] (US; blue eyes)

brights [1970s] (US Black)

daylights [mid-18C+]

day-opener [mid–late 19C] (orig. boxing)

deadlights [19C]

deuce of peekers [1940s]

eeks [1950s+]

front windows [mid-19C]

gagers/gaggers [19C] (US)

ooooooooooooooooooooooooooooooooo
Bulging and squinting eyes

bug-eye [20C] (a round or bulging eye)

bung eyes [20C] (US; protruding eyes)

cock-eye [mid-19C] (a squinting eye)

eye-limpet [late 19C] (an artificial eye)

fofi-eye [20C] (W.I./Bdos., Guyn.; an eye with a
   discoloured, whitish eyeball)

highbeams [1980s+] (drugs; the wide eyes of a
   person on crack cocaine)

squinny-eyes [late 17C–mid-19C] (squinting eyes)

squinter [late 19C] (a squinting eye)

ooooooooooooooooooooooooooooooooo

gig [1920s] (US)

gig-lamps [mid-19C+] (from the two lights placed to either side of a gig or light carriage)

gims [1940s] (US Black)

glasiers/glaziers/glasyers [mid-16C–18C]

glim/glym [late 18C+]

goggles

glimmer/glimmar/glymmer [19C] (US)

glimmers [late 18C+]

goggler [early–mid-19C]

goggles [early 18C–early 19C]

The eyes in rhyming slang

jam pies [1990s]

Joan Baez [1960s–70s]

lamb's fries [20C] (Aus.)

meat pies [20C]

minces/mince pies [mid-19C+]

mud pies [20C] (Aus.)

mutton-pies [19C]

nellies/nelly blighs [1910s+] (Aus.)

pies [1940s] (US Black)

porkies/porky pies [20C]

puddings and pies [mid-19C]

sargent's pies [1940s–50s] (Aus.)

headlamps [1970s+] (US)

headlights [late 19C+] (US)

immies [1940s+] (US; a type of marble)

killers [late 18C]

lamp [19C+]

langtries [late 19C] (attractive eyes, from Lillie *Langtry*, a
    beauty and popular singer)

lights [early 19C+]

lookers [20C] (US)

oglers [early 19C]

ogles [late 17C+]

optics [17C+]

peekers [1940s] (US Black)

peepers [late 17C+]

peeps [mid-19C]

pumps [19C]

rum ogles [late 17C–mid-19C] (UK Und.; bright, clear eyes)

saucers [mid-19C]

seers [19C]

sees [late 18C–early 19C] (UK Und.)

shutters [1940s] (US Black)

slanters [1940s] (US Black)

sparklers [mid-18C–mid-19C] (bright or sparkling eyes)

spotters [1940s] (US Black)

spies [19C]

toplights [18C]

twinklers [19C+]

windows [mid-19C]

winkers [late 19C]

○○○○○○○○○○○○○○○○○○○○○○○○○○○○○○○○○
Bags

coal [1990s] (Aus.; dark bags under the eyes)

luggage [1970s] (US teen: bags under the eyes)

○○○○○○○○○○○○○○○○○○○○○○○○○○○○○○○○○

Black eyes

beefer/beef eye [20C]

blinker [mid-19C+] (orig. US)

Botany Bay coat-of-arms [early–mid-19C] (Aus.; a broken nose and black eyes)

bruiser [late 16C+] (US)

bung [late 19C+]

bunger [1900s–30s] (US)

casualty [late 19C–1900s]

colonial livery [19C] (Aus.; a bloody nose and a black eye)

cranberry eye [late 19C] (US; a bloodshot eye)

deep grief [late 19C] (a pair of blackened eyes)

eyes like pissholes in the snow [20C] (orig. milit.; deeply sunken bloodshot eyes)

goog [1920s–30s] (US)

half-a-surprise [late 19C–1900s] (a single black eye, from Charles Coborn's song lyric (c.1886), 'Two lovely black eyes/Oh what a surprise')

half-mourning [mid-19C] (a single black eye)

Irishman's coat of arms [mid-18C–mid-19C]

Monday mouse [late 19C] (a black eye, resulting from a Saturday or Sunday night (drunken) fight)

morris minor [20C] (a black eye; rhy. sl. 'shiner')

mouse [mid-19C+] (?orig. US)

mouser [mid-19C+]

Northumberland arms/Lord
   Northumberland's arms [late 17C– late 18C]

painted peeper [19C]

peepers in mourning [19C] (a pair of black eyes)

shiner [19C+] (Und.)

stinker [early 19C–1950s]

○○○○○○○○○○○○○○○○○○○○○○○○○○○○○○○○○○○○○

THE EARS

cabbage leaves [20C] (US)

ear flap [mid-19C–1930s] (US)

earhole [1920s+]

flap [1950s]

flappers [1930s+] (US)

flaps [1960s+]

flaptabs [1950s+]

flippers [1900s–40s] (US Black)

harker [mid-19C] (US)

hearing cheats [mid-16C–19C] (UK Und.)

horn [1940s+]

listener [early 19C+] (orig. boxing)
lug [late 16C+]
lughole [20C]
mikes [1940s] (US Black)
sails [1940s] (US Black)
tab [mid-19C+]

jug-handles

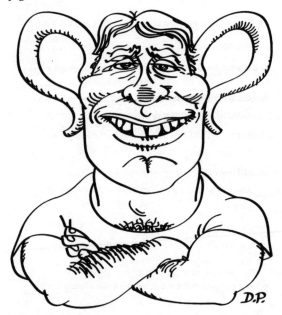

○○○○○○○○○○○○○○○○○○○○○○○○○○○○○○○○○
The ear in rhyming slang

Rhyming with 'ear'

bottle of beer [20C]

glass of beer [late 19C+]

King Lear [late 19C+]

Melbourne Pier/Port Melbourne Pier
[1940s+] (Aus.)

Southend pier [20C]

Rhyming with 'lug'

toby jug [20C]

○○○○○○○○○○○○○○○○○○○○○○○○○○○○○○○○○

○○○○○○○○○○○○○○○○○○○○○○○○○○○○○○○○○
Cauliflower and misshapen ears

bakore [1970s+] (S. Afr.; large, protruding ears;
lit. 'bowl ears')

cauliflower [1940s+] (a boxer's ear which has
taken too many punches to retain its original
shape)

jug-handles/jug-lugs [20C] (sticking out ears)

thick ear [late 19C+] (an ear that has swollen up
after a blow)

○○○○○○○○○○○○○○○○○○○○○○○○○○○○○○○○○

taps [mid-18C–mid-19C]

wattles [late 18C–mid-19C]

yarker [late 19C–1900s]

THE NOSE

air hook [20C] (US)

bacca-box [1900s–20s]

beagle [1920s–30s] (US)

beak [early 18C+]

beezer [20C] (orig. boxing)

○○○○○○○○○○○○○○○○○○○○○○○○○○○○○○○○

The nose in rhyming slang

Rhyming with 'nose'

Irish rose [20C]

ruby rose [20C]

suppose/I suppose [mid-19C+]

Tokyo rose [1940s–50s]

Rhyming with 'conk'

glass of plonk [20C]

Rhyming with 'snout'

in-and-out [20C]

salmon and trout [20C]

○○○○○○○○○○○○○○○○○○○○○○○○○○○○○○○○

○○

Red noses

bardolph [1990s]

beacon [late 19C]

brandy blossom [late 19C]

danger light/danger signal [20C]

fiery snorter [mid-19C]

geranium [late 19C]

gin blossom [1930s] (US)

nase nab/nazy nab [late 17C–early 19C]

old raspberry [1910s–20s]

rudolph [1990s]

strawberry [late 19C]

○○

bill [early–mid-19C+] (US)

boke [mid-19C] (US)

boko [mid-19C+]

bowsprit [late 17C–19C]

bracket [1950s+]

bugle [early 19C+]

claret-jug [mid-19C]

foghorn [20C]

gig [late 17C–early 19C]

gnomon [late 16C–early 19C] (from a type of timepiece that indicates the time of day by casting its shadow on a marked surface)

handle [18C–mid-19C]

handle of one's face [early 18C]

Harry James [1950s] (the name of a famous trumpet player and bandleader)

honker [1940s+]

hooter [1950s+]

○○○○○○○○○○○○○○○○○○○○○○○○○○○○○○○○○
Large, hooked and other unusual noses

banana-nose [1920s+] (US)

briar-root [late 19C] (an ill-shaped, battered nose)

celestial [mid–late 19C] (a turned-up nose)

cheese-cutter [mid-19C] (an aquiline nose)

cherry-picker [20C] (US)

cowcatcher [1940s–50s]

dook [mid–late 19C] (*duke*, from the Duke of Wellington, renowned for his large nose)

nutcrackers [late 19C–1900s] (a hooked nose and a prominent chin)

parish pick-axe [late 19C]

○○○○○○○○○○○○○○○○○○○○○○○○○○○○○○○○○

horn [mid-19C+]

leading article [mid–late 19C]

muzzle [15C+]

neb [late 19C+]

nozzle [mid-18C+]

paste-horn [19C]

peak [19C]

post-horn [19C]

proboscis [mid-17C+]

razzo [late 19C–1930s]

schnozzle [1940s+] (German *Schnauze*, a snout)

schnozzola [1950s+]

sensitive plant [early–mid-19C] (orig. boxing)

sensitive truncheon [19C]

shonk [20C]

smeller [late 17C–1900s]

smelling-cheat [16C–early 19C]

sneeze [19C–1910s]

sneezer [early 18C–mid-19C]

sniffer [mid-19C+]

snifter [19C]

snitch [mid-17C+]

snoot [mid-19C+]

snorer [mid-19C–1950s]

snorter [early 19C+]

snot [18C]

snot-box [20C]

snot-locker [1980s] (US)

snotter [mid-19C]

snottle-box [19C]

snozzle [1930s+]

snuff-box [early–mid-19C]

snuffer [1940s] (US Black)

snuffle [early–mid-19C]

spectacles-seat [late 19C]

trumpet [19C]

THE MOUTH

bacca-box [1900s–20s]

bazoo [late 19C–1940s]

beak [early 18C+]

blab [early 17C+]

blabber [16C]

blowhole [1940s] (US)

blubber [late 18C] (UK Und.)

bone box [late 18C–mid-19C]

boose [20C] (US)

box [1930s–50s] (US)

box of dominoes [mid-19C]

box of ivories [mid-19C]

bunghole [17C; 1930s+] (Aus.)

busser [mid-19C] (US, lit. 'kisser')

cap [1960s–70s]

chaffer [19C]

chapper [late 19C]

chirper [19C+]

clack-box [19C]

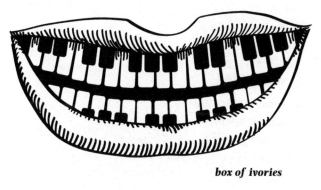

box of ivories

clacker [19C]

clam [early 19C–1950s]

clamshell [early–mid-19C] (US)

clamtrap [early 19C–1940s] (US)

clapper [1930s+]

clap-trap [1960s–70s]

cocksucker [1940s+] (US)

domino-box [19C]

dribbler [19C]

dubber [18C–19C]

Dutch oven [1920s]

face [mid-19C+]

fag-hole [1940s+]

flap [1950s+] (US)

flapper [1930s+] (US Black)

flatter-trap [mid-19C]

flytrap [18C+]

gab [18C+]

gab-box [20C] (US)

gan [16C–19C]

gap [late 19C+]

○○○○○○○○○○○○○○○○○○○○○○○○○○○○○○○○○
The mouth in rhyming slang
east and south [mid-19C]

north and south [mid-19C+]

queen of the south [20C]

salmon and trout [mid-19C+]

salmon trout [mid-19C]

sunny south [late 19C]

○○○○○○○○○○○○○○○○○○○○○○○○○○○○○○○○○

○○○○○○○○○○○○○○○○○○○○○○○○○○○○○○○○○○○○○○○

Large mouths

oven [late 18C–mid-19C]

satch [1900s–40s] (US Black)

satchel-mouth [1900s–40s]

sparrow-mouth [late 17C–1900s]

spout [late 19C]

○○○○○○○○○○○○○○○○○○○○○○○○○○○○○○○○○○○○○○○

gapper [1980s+] (US)

garret [late 19C]

gash [mid-19C] (US)

gate [1930s+]

gazebo [1900s] (US)

gig [mid–late 19C]

gob [mid-16C+]

gobber [1920s–30s]

graveyard [19C]

grill [1980s+] (US Black/teen)

hatch [1920s+] (US, orig. naut.)

hatchway [early–mid-19C]

head [mid-19C+] (US)

hole [late 14C+]

hopper [mid-19C–1910s]

jawing-tackle [early–mid-19C]

jib [20C]

jug [early 19C+]

kisser [mid-19C+]

kissing-trap [19C] (orig. boxing)

○○○○○○○○○○○○○○○○○○○○○○○○○○○○○○○○○○○
A place for food and drink

bacon hole [1940s+]

beer street [mid-19C]

bread trap [mid-19C] (US)

bun-trap [20C]

cakehole [1940s+]

coffee-mill [19C]

feed box [20C]

feeder [1900s–20s] (US)

gingerbread-trap [mid-19C]

gin lane [mid-19C]

gin-trap [early 19C]

gobbler [19C]

grub-box [mid-19C]

grub-mill [late 19C] (US)

grub-shop [mid-19C]

grub-trap [mid-19C]

meat trap [mid–late 19C+] (Aus./US)

pie hole [1990s]

porridge hole [late 19C] (Scot.)

potato-box [late 18C]

potato jaw [late 18C]

potato-trap [late 18C–late 19C]

saucebox [mid-19C+]

tater-trap [mid-19C–1910s]

tattie-trap [late 19C]

○○○○○○○○○○○○○○○○○○○○○○○○○○○○○○○○○

laughing gear [1970s+]

lung-box [mid–late 19C]

maw [mid-19C+]

moey/mooe/mooey [late 19C+]

mousetrap [late 19C+]

mummer [late 18C–early 19C]

mums [late 18C–late 19C]

mun/mund/munn/munne [14C–late 19C]

muzzle [15C+]

napper [late 17C–18C]

neb [late 17C–early 19C]

nib [late 18C–mid-19C]

patterer [19C]

prater [19C]

clamshells

○○○○○○○○○○○○○○○○○○○○○○○○○○○○○○○○○○
The lips in rhyming slang
apple pips [1900s–20s]
P.G. tips [20C]

○○○○○○○○○○○○○○○○○○○○○○○○○○○○○○○○○○

prattler [19C]

rag box/rag shop [late 19C]

rattletrap [19C]

rat trap [late 19C+]

rosebud [late 19C+]

screech [1970s+]

shop [mid–late 19C]

sluice(-house) [mid-19C–1920s]

smush [1930s] (US)

spoke-box [19C]

talk-trap [20C]

trap [late 18C+]

whistle [late 14C+]

wordhole [1990s] (US)

yap [late 19C+]

THE LIPS

chops [18C+]

clamshells [mid-19C] (US)

coffee coolers [1950s] (US Black; esp. large and protuberant lips)

fangs [1950s–60s] (US Black/jazz)

ganns [late 17C–18C]

jibs [20C]

liver-chops [mid-19C] (large, dark lips)

liver-lips [1910s+] (US Black; large, dark lips)

rubies [1940s] (US Black)

sweeteners [late 19C] (UK Und.)

THE TONGUE

baking-spittle [late 19C] (Lancashire/Yorks.; a type of thin board used in baking cakes)

chaffer [19C]

clack [late 16C–mid-19C]

clapper [mid-17C–mid-19C]

glib [mid-18C]

jib [mid-19C]

lapper [mid-19C]

licker [1970s+]

manchester [early 19C]

melt [20C]

○○○○○○○○○○○○○○○○○○○○○○○○○○○○○○○○○○○
The tongue in rhyming slang
first of May [mid–late 19C] ('say')

heart and lung [1920s] (US)

Jimmy Young [20C]

○○○○○○○○○○○○○○○○○○○○○○○○○○○○○○○○○○○

mouth organ [late 19C–1920s]

prating cheat [mid-16C–mid-19C]

prattling-cheat [16C]

rag [early 19C+]

red flannel [19C]

red rag [late 17C–late 19C]

unruly member [19C]

velvet [late 17C–19C]

THE TEETH

biters [1930s–40s] (US)

bones [19C]

box of worries [19C]

bread-cutters/butter-grinders [20C] (US)

cage of ivories [late 18C]

chalkies [mid-19C] (US)

chatterers [early 19C–1900s]

chewers [1940s]

chiclets [1950s+] (US)

china [1940s+] (US)

chompers [20C] (US)

choppers [1940s+]

corn-grinders [mid-19C] (US)

crackers [1930s+]

○○○○○○○○○○○○○○○○○○○○○○○○○○○○○○○○○○
False teeth

cheaters [1920s+] (orig. US)

china choppers [1940s+]

china clippers [1950s+] (US)

clackers [1930s+]

clickers [20C]

clompers [20C] (US)

deadman choppers/deadman teeth
[20C] (US Black)

dentals [20C] (US)

falsies [1940s+]

plumbing [1930s–50s] (fillings in teeth)

shop teeth [20C] (Irish)

snappers [1920s–50s]

○○○○○○○○○○○○○○○○○○○○○○○○○○○○○○○○○○

crashing-cheats/crassing cheats [mid-16C–mid-19C]
(UK Und.)

crockery [1910s–1940s] (US)

crumb-crusher [1940s–70s] (US Black)

curls [early 19C]

dining room furniture [early 19C]

dinner-set [late 19C]

dominoes [late 19C]

eating tackle [20C]

fangs [mid-19C+]

grinders [late 17C+]

head rails [mid-18C–mid-19C]

ivories [late 18C+]

lispers [late 18C–mid-19C]

mompyns/munpins [mid-15C] (lit. 'mouth-pins')

nutcrackers [late 19C–1900s]

park-palings/park-railings [early–mid-19C]

○○○○○○○○○○○○○○○○○○○○○○○○○○○○○○○○
The teeth in rhyming slang

Rhyming with 'teeth' or 'tooth'

Bexley Heath [late 19C+]

General Booth [20C]

hampsteads/hamps [mid-19C+] (i.e. *Hampstead* Heath)

Hounslow Heath [mid-19C]

roast beef [20C]

Ted Heath [1970s]

underbeneaths [20C] (US)

Rhyming with 'tats'

cricket bats [20C] (Aus.)

○○○○○○○○○○○○○○○○○○○○○○○○○○○○○○○○

pearlies [late 19C+]

pearly gates [1960s–70s]

pearly-whites [1970s+] (orig. US)

peggies [late 19C+]

pots [1980s+] (Polari)

railings [mid-19C–1910s]

rattlers [19C]

○○○○○○○○○○○○○○○○○○○○○○○○○○○○○○○○○○○○
Buck teeth

bread-and-butter teeth [20C]

butter bean teeth [20C]

butter teeth [20C] (US)

franklin teeth [1920s–30s] (Can.; from the
protruding grille of the *Franklin* automobile)

gravestones [20C] (US)

rabbit teeth [early 19C]

snaggs [late 18C–early 19C] (large teeth)

snags [1910s+] (Aus.; jagged teeth)

tombstones [mid-19C–1900s] (crooked teeth)

tush-teeth [20C] (W.I.)

○○○○○○○○○○○○○○○○○○○○○○○○○○○○○○○○○○○○

tombstones

rocks [20C]

stumps [19C+]

tats/tatts [1900s–10s]

toothy-pegs [early 19C+] (usu. juv.)

uppers and downers [1950s–60s]

THE CHIN

Andy Gump [1920s+] (a conspicuously receding chin)

Andy McGinn [1930s–50s] (rhy. sl.)

button [19C+]

chillers [20C] (a double chin)

Errol Flynn [1940s+] (rhy. sl.)

Gunga Din [20C] (rhy. sl.)

saving chin [late 18C–mid-19C] (a protruding chin)

thick and thin [20C] (rhy. sl.)

underwear [1960s+] (an unshaven chin)

Vera Lynn [1940s+] (rhy. sl.)

THE NECK

bushel and peck [late 19C+] (rhy. sl.)

col [16C]

colquarron [late 17C–mid-19C] (?French *col*, a neck + *quarrom*, a body)

Gregory Peck [1950s+] (rhy. sl.)

necklace [17C]

nub [late 17C–early 19C]

scrag [18C]

squeeze [19C]

squeezer [mid-19C]

three quarters of a peck [mid-19C] (rhy. sl.)

THE THROAT

beer street [mid-19C]

bolt [mid-19C]

chaffer [19C]

common sewer [19C]

drain [19C]

feeder [1900s–20s] (US)

funnel [18C]

gan [16C–19C]

gargler [late 19C]

gin lane [mid-19C]

gizzard [mid-19C–1930s]

gorrel [1980s+] (S. Afr.)

gozzle [1900s–70s] (US)

gully (hole) [19C]

gutter lane [late 17C–18C]

guzzle [late 17C+]

hatch [1920s+] (US, orig. naut.)

°°°°°°°°°°°°°°°°°°°°°°°°°°°°°°°°°°

The Adam's apple

forbidden fruit [1930s–40s] (Irish)

goozle [19C+]

rum-bump [1950s]

°°°°°°°°°°°°°°°°°°°°°°°°°°°°°°°°°°

Irish channel [1900s]

lane [mid-16C+]

nanny (goat) [20C] (rhy. sl.)

narrow lane [mid-16C]

organ-pipe [mid-19C–1920s]

peck alley [mid-19C]

pipes [16C+]

quail pipe [late 17C–18C]

red lane [late 18C+]

red lion lane [mid-19C]

screech [1970s+]

sink-hole [mid–late 19C]

spew alley [mid-19C–1900s]

spud-grinder [1970s]

swallow [19C]

swallow-pipe [20C]

throttle [14C+]

whistle [late 14C+]

wicket [19C]

THE ARM(S)

bender [mid-19C+]

brace of hookers [late 19C–1940s] (US Black)

fin [late 18C+]

○○○○○○○○○○○○○○○○○○○○○○○○○○○○○○○○○○○○
The arms in rhyming slang
burglar alarm [20C]

Chalk (Farm) [mid-19C–1910s]

Emmerdale (Farm) [1970s+]

false alarm [20C] (orig. milit.)

fire-alarms [20C]

five-acre farm [mid-19C]

Indian charm [20C]

lucky charm [20C]

Warwick Farm [1940s–60s] (Aus.)

○○○○○○○○○○○○○○○○○○○○○○○○○○○○○○○○○○○○

flappers [mid-19C; 1930s–40s]

flipper [mid-19C+]

gun [1980s+] (US)

hoop-stick [late 19C]

martinis [1980s+] (gay)

meathook [mid–late 19C] (Aus./US)

prop [late 18C–late 19C]

rammer [late 18C–19C]

smiter [late 17C–early 19C]

wing [early 19C+]

forks

THE HAND(S)

axholder [late 19C] (US)

biscuit hooks [1930s] (US)

biscuit snatchers [1940s–60s] (US Black)

bread hooks [20C] (US)

breadsnatchers [1960s] (US)

bunch of five(s) [19C+] (a fist)

clam-diggers [20C] (US)

clampers/clamps [late 19C+] (US)

clams [1960s] (US)

claw [mid-18C+]

clutch [late 18C]

cock-scratchers [1970s]

cornstealer [mid-19C]

cotton-pickers [1960s+] (US)

crumb-snatchers [20C]

daddle [late 18C–late 19C]

daddler [late 19C]

deenach [mid-19C+] (backslang)

dexter [late 18C–early 19C]

fam/famm/fem/feme [18C+]

famble [16C+]

feeler [late 19C]

fin [late 18C+]

fish-hook [1920s+]

fives [17C]

flapper [19C]

flapper-shaker [19C]

flesh hooks [17C]

flipper [mid-19C+]

flippers [late 19C+] (US)

forefoot [16C]

forks [late 19C+]

frigger [late 17C]

German comb [late 19C+] (US)

glom/glaum [1930s+] (US)

goll [late 16C–early 17C]

grab [1900s–30s] (US)

grabber [mid-19C+]

○○○○○○○○○○○○○○○○○○○○○○○○○○○○○○○○○

The hands in rhyming slang

Rhyming with 'hand(s)'

brass band [20C]

German bands [20C]

Margate sands [20C]

Martin-le-Grand [mid–late 19C]

mary ann [20C]

Ramsgate sands [20C]

St Martin's (le Grand) [mid-19C–1940s]
(a London street name)

Rhyming with 'fork'

dook [mid–late 19C] (i.e. *duke* of York)

duke [mid-19C+] (i.e. *duke* of York)

Rhyming with 'fin'

Lincoln's Inn [mid-19C+]

○○○○○○○○○○○○○○○○○○○○○○○○○○○○○○○○○

grabbers [early 19C+]

grabhooks [1910s–40s] (US)

grappler [mid-19C]

grapples [mid–late 19C]

grappling hooks [late 19C–1910s] (US)

gropers [19C]

grub hooks [1920s+] (US)

hook [early 19C+]

jelly snatchers [1970s] (US Black)

knucks [mid-19C–1950s] (the *knuck*les)

lillies [1910s–30s] (US)

lilywhites [1920s–70s]

lunch hooks [late 19C+] (orig. US)

mauler [early 19C+] (the fist)

mauley/maulie/mawley/morley [early 19C+]

meathooks [1910s+] (US/Aus.)

mitt [19C] (US)

mitten [19C+]

mud hook [early 19C+] (Aus./US)

nippers [early–mid-19C] (US)

paddle [mid-19C+]

palette [late 18C–mid-19C]

paw [late 17C+]

picker [mid-19C]

pickers [1940s] (US Black)

pickers and stealers [17C+]

plier/plyer [mid-late 19C] (UK Und.)

prayer-dukes/prayer-handles [1920s–40s] (US Black)

props [late 18C–19C]

pudsey/pudsy [17C] (?Dutch *poot*, a paw)

scratcher [early–mid-19C]

shaker [mid-19C]

skin [1930s+] (US Black)

southpaw [mid-19C+] (orig. US baseball; the left hand)

spud [mid–late 19C] (a baby's hand)

tools [mid-19C–1900s]

THE FINGERS

bunch of sprouts [19C]

claw [mid-18C+]

claws [17C+]

cunt-hooks/twat-hooks [20C]

digitals [mid-19C]

divers [late 19C+]

dog dinger [1920s–70s] (US Black; the middle or index finger)

feelers [late 19C]

fish-hooks [late 18C+]

flanges [mid-19C]

fork-hooks [20C] (US)

forks [18C–early 19C; US Black 1940s] (orig. UK; the middle and forefingers)

grabbers [early 19C+]

grabhooks [1910s–40s] (US)

grapplers [mid-19C]

grappling irons/grapplings [mid-19C]

grappling hooks [late 19C–1910s] (US)

grub hooks [1920s+] (US)

hooks [early 19C+]

lickpot [20C] (the index finger)

lunch hooks [late 19C+] (orig. US)

meathooks [1910s+]

muck-forks [mid-19C]

○○○○○○○○○○○○○○○○○○○○○○○○○○○○○○○○
Five fingers and one thumb in rhyming slang

bees wingers [1960s+]

bell ringers [20C]

Jamaica rum [20C]

lean and lingers [1920s]

onka [1960s+] (Aus.: i.e. *Onka*paringa, the brand-name of a make of woollen blanket)

wait and lingers [20C]

○○○○○○○○○○○○○○○○○○○○○○○○○○○○○○○○

○○○○○○○○○○○○○○○○○○○○○○○○○○○○○○○○○
The hands and fingers
as aids to masturbation

button finger [1990s]

five-finger mary [1970s+]

Guru Palm and the five pillars of wisdom
   [1990s+]

**mary fist/mary ellen/mary five-fingers/mary
   palm** [1940s+] (US)

minnie five fingers [1920s] (US)

Miss Fist [20C]

**Mother Fist and her five daughters/Mother
   Five Fingers** [20C]

Mr Palmer and his five sons [1950s+] (gay)

Mrs Palm(er) and her five daughters [1950s+]

Mrs. Hand and her five daughters [1950s+]

Pam and her five sisters [1990s]

rosy palm and her five (little) sisters [20C]

wanking spanners [1920s+]

○○○○○○○○○○○○○○○○○○○○○○○○○○○○○○○○○

mud hook [1920s+]

nimbles [early 17C]

nippers [early–mid-19C]

paddle [mid-19C+]

pinkies [19C]

pinky [early 19C+] (the little finger)

poppers [1940s]

stealers/ten stealers [mid-17C]

stink-finger [late 19C+] (the middle finger)

ten bones [late 15C–early 16C; 1940s]

ten commandments [mid-15C–mid-19C] (a woman's fingers and thumbs)

thieving hooks [early 19C]

ticklers [20C]

wigglers [1940s]

wanking spanners

TO GESTICULATE

bite one's thumb [late 16C–late 17C] (to make a gesture of contempt or of threat)

bump start [20C] (to make a violent gesture or action)

do hooky [mid–late 19C] (to make the coarse gesture of applying the thumb and fingers to one's nose)

give the fig [late 16C–early 19C] (to stick one's thumb up between two forefingers as a gesture of derision)

have a sight at [mid-19C] (to make a rude gesture, i.e. 'to place the thumb against the nose ... closing all the fingers except the little one, which is agitated in token of derision')

highball [1920s–30s] (to make a gesture with one's hand)

make a long nose [mid-19C] (to thumb one's nose)

pull bacon [mid-19C+] (to thumb one's nose)

smell your mother [1990s] (an insult, usu. accompanied by waving the middle finger under the insultee's nose; the implication is of recent sexual foreplay)

take a (double) sight [mid-19C] (to place the thumb against the nose and close all the fingers except the little one, which is agitated as a token of derision)

take a grinder [mid-19C] (to make a coarse gesture similar to thumbing one's nose and using the other hand to work an imaginary coffee-grinder)

°°°°°°°°°°°°°°°°°°°°°°°°°°°°°°°°°°°°°°
Giving the finger and making V

do a Harvey Smith [1970s+] (from the
showjumper *Harvey Smith*, who outraged the
staid world of showjumping by making a V-sign
gesture in public)

**flag the bone/flip the bone/give the
bone/shoot the bone** [1960s+] (US)

flip off [1960s+]

flip the bird [1950s+]

give someone the finger [1960s+]

make V [early 17C]

°°°°°°°°°°°°°°°°°°°°°°°°°°°°°°°°°°°°°°

GESTURES

big razzoo [1930s+] (a gesture of extreme contempt or scorn)

bird [1960s+] (US; an obscene gesture of dismissal, mockery)

bump start [20C] (a violent gesture or action)

fig (of Spain) [late 16C–19C] (a coarse gesture of dismissal
whereby one sticks one's thumb up between two forefingers)

finger [late 19C+] (an obscene gesture of contempt)

fuck-off [1940s+] (a gesture of contempt)

hang it in your ass! [1950s+] (US; an excl. of contempt, accompanied by a gesture, the right forefinger is hooked over the left
thumb, which in turn makes a circle with the left forefinger)

Italian salute [1940s+] (US; an obscene gesture of contempt
  or derision; one arm is bent and the fist and forearm thrust
  upwards while the other hand grasps the forearm or bicep)
jailhouse salute [1970s] (an obscene gesture)
one-finger(ed) salute [1960s+] (an obscene gesture of
  contempt)

TO SHAKE HANDS

duke [mid-19C–1920s]
fam-grasp [late 17C–18C]
give someone one's fist [early 19C–1900s]
have dook on it [20C] (Aus.)
mitt [1900s–50s]
press the flesh [1920s+]
pump the stump [1940s]
pump-handle [mid–late 19C]
slang the mauleys [late 18C–late 19C]
sling a daddle [late 19C]
sling one's mauley [19C]
tip one's fin [late 18C–late 19C]
tip the daddle [late 18C–late 19C]
tip the gripes in a dangle/tip the gripes in a tangle [late
  18C–late 19C]
whip out [20C]

THE TORSO

apple-cart [18C+]

beer barrel [19C]

birthday suit [mid-18C+] (the naked body)

bod [late 18C+]

bone-house [19C]

buddy [mid-19C+] (W.I./UK Black teen)

carrion [late 18C]

chassis [1930s+]

classy chassis [1950s–60s] (US; the body of a good-looking, well-built woman)

European accentuation [1950s+] (gay; a tapered body with jutting buttocks)

four bones [1920s] (Irish)

frame [1940s–50s] (orig. US Black)

left raise [1930s–40s] (US Black; the left-hand side of one's body plus the relevant limbs)

ooooooooooooooooooooooooooooooo
The body in rhyming slang

hot toddy [20C]

leucoddy [mid-19C+] (Polari)

tom noddy [20C]

ooooooooooooooooooooooooooooooo

live blanket [1990s] (a human body, particularly when covering another, as in sexual intercourse)

meat [late 16C+]

mutton [late 18C–late 19C] (US)

ninepins [late 19C]

physical [1990s]

piece [late 18C+]

soul-case [late 18C-early 19C]

structure [1950s+]

THE LUNGS

air bags [1940s+] (US Black/Harlem)

bagpipes [early–mid-19C]

bellers [18C–1920s] (Cockney pron. of 'bellows')

bellows [18C–1920s]

breathers [1910s]

cat's meat [early–19C+]

pipes [16C+] (orig. US Black)

vacuum cleaners [1940s] (US Black)

windbags/wind-pumps [mid-19C–1940s] (US Black)

THE HEART

carburettor [1920s]

chimer [1940s] (US Black)

clock [mid-19C+] (US Black)

dicky ticker [late 19C+] (a weak heart)

gizzard [mid-19C–1930s] (US)

panter [late 18C–early 19C]

pump [20C]

ticker [19C]

○○○○○○○○○○○○○○○○○○○○○○○○○○○○○○○○○○
The heart in rhyming slang

Rhyming with 'heart'

gooseberry tart [mid-19C–1930s]

grocer's cart [20C] (Aus.)

horse and cart [late 19C]

jam tart [20C]

raspberry tart [late 19C+]

stop and start [20C]

strawberry tart [1960s+]

Rhyming with 'pump'

skip and jump [20C]

○○○○○○○○○○○○○○○○○○○○○○○○○○○○○○○○○○

THE BREASTS

baby bumpers [1960s+]

baps [1990s] (orig. Ulster)

bazoombas [1080s+] (US)

bibble chunks [1990s]

bongos [1980s+] (US)

boob [1940s+] (orig. US)

boobies [1930s+] (orig. US)

bouncers [1950s–70s]

B.S.H.'s [1960s–70s] (*B*ritish *S*tandard *H*andfuls)

bubbies [17C]

charlies [mid-19C+]

Charlie Wheelers [1940s+] (Aus.: from *Charles Wheeler*, a
   painter of nudes)

charms [mid-19C+]

credentials [1960s+] (US)

filthy pillows [1990s]

fleshy bagpipes [1990s]

forebuttocks [early 18C]

fuck udders [1990s]

globes [19C+]

hand-warmers [1920s+] (Aus.)

headlights [20C]

hooters [1970s+] (US)

johnsons [1970s] (US)

jugs [1950s] (orig. US)

knockers [1930s+] (orig. US)

lung warts [1940s+] (US)

mammaries [1970s+]

maracas [1940s+] (US)

○○○○○○○○○○○○○○○○○○○○○○○○○○○○○○○○○○
The breasts in rhyming slang

Rhyming with 'tits' or 'titties'

Bradford cities [1990s]

Brad Pitts/bradleys [1990s]

Bristols [1960s+] (i.e. *Bristol* bits)

cats and kitties [mid-20C]

fainting fits [1940s+]

tale of two cities [1950s]

thousand pities [late 19C–1900s]

threepenny bits [late 19C+]

thrups [late 19C+] (i.e. '*thrup*enny bits')

Rhyming with 'breasts'

cabman's rests [late 19C+]

Rhyming with 'knockers'

mods and rockers [1960s]

○○○○○○○○○○○○○○○○○○○○○○○○○○○○○○○○○○

udders

milk bottles [1930s+] (Aus.)

nice pair of eyes [1960s+]

norks [1950s+] (Aus.: from *Norco* Ltd. butter manufacturer in NSW)

nubbies [late 19C+] (Aus.)

panters [late 19C–1900s]

plumpies [1990s]

puppies [1990s]

shock-absorbers [1950s+]

swingers [1920s+] (Aus.)

tits [17C+]

tooraloorals [late 19C]

udders [1930s+]

upper deck [1940s] (Aus.)

waps/wap-waps [1990s] (lit. 'shakers')

THE NIPPLES

berries [1970s+] (US Black)

buttons [1960s] (US)

chapel hat pegs [20C]

kittens' noses [1990s]

nips [1970s+] (US)

raspberries [1970s+]

THE BACK

hammer (and tack) [1950s+] (rhy. sl.)

last card of the pack [mid-19C–1910s] (rhy. sl.)

lumberjack [20C] (rhy. sl.)

penny black [20C] (rhy. sl.)

union jack [20C] (rhy. sl.)

THE BELLY

baggage-room [mid-19C] (US)

basket [late 19C+]

bearings [20C] (Aus.)

beer barrel [19C]

bingy [mid-19C+] (Aus./N.Z.)

boiler [1920s–60s] (US)

bread-bag [mid-19C]

breadbasket [early 19C+] (orig. boxing)

bread box [1910s] (US)

clam-basket [early 19C] (US)

commissary department [late 19C–1900s] (US)

crammer [mid–late 19C]

craw [late 16C–early 19C]

crib [mid-17C]

cupboard [mid-19C] (US)

depressed area [1930s+]

dumpling depot [mid-19C]

gizzard [mid-19C–1930s]

gormy-ruddles [19C] (*gormy-ruttles*, quinsy in horses)

grill [1940s] (US Black)

grubbery [19C]

guts [late 14C+]

Holloway, Middlesex [mid-19C–1900s] (punning on both
   locations)

inner man [mid-19C]

inside [mid-18C+]

keg [late 19C+]

kishkes [20C] (Yiddish, 'intestines')

oooooooooooooooooooooooooooooooo

Fat bellies

bay window [mid–late 19C]

beer pot [1980s+]

booze balloon [1970s+] (N.Z.)

booze belly [20C] (US)

bow-window [early 19C+]

double guts [20C] (US)

doughbelly [1940s+] (US)

goodyear [1960s+] (i.e. 'spare tyre')

handles [1980s+] (US campus)

idleset [20C] (Ulster)

love handles [1960s+]

pod [late 19C–1910s]

pot [20C]

pus-gut/pustle-gut [20C]

puzzlegut [1900s–40s] (US Black)

saddle bags [1960s+]

spare tyre [1920s+]

tenpenny [1940s] (W.I.)

oooooooooooooooooooooooooooooooo

The belly in rhyming slang

Rhyming with 'belly'

cape kelly [1940s] (Aus.)

darby kelly [late 19C+]

Ned Kelly [1920s+]

New Delhi [20C]

Rhyming with 'guts'

comic cuts [1940s+]

newington butts [20C]

kitchen [late 19C+]

kite [mid-16C–early 17C]

labonza [1930s+] (US; Italian *la pancia*, the stomach)

little mary [1900s–20s]

locker [mid-19C+] (US)

lunch-basket [1910s]

lunchbox [1970s] (US Black)

meatbag [19C]

middle piece/middle pie [mid-19C–1900s]

pail [1940s] (US Black)

pantry [20C] (US)

pipkin [mid-19C]

porridge bowl [mid-19C–1900s]

pudding [late 17C+]

pudding-house [late 16C+]

puku [20C] (N.Z.)

shitbag [late 19C–1910s]

tranklement [19C]

trollobubs/trollybobs [19C]

tum [mid-19C+]

tum-jack [1940s–50s]

water-butt/water-barrel [late 19C]

works [late 19C–1900s] (US)

oooooooooooooooooooooooooooooooo
Stomach-ache

belly-ache [mid-19C+]

belly-grunting [1920s+] (Aus.)

belly vengeance [mid-19C]

collywobbles [mid-19C]

gollywobbles [1940s+] (US)

granny grunt/granny chills [20C] (US)

gripes [mid-19C]

gutache [early 19C+]

heaves [late 19C+]

wiffle-woffles [mid-19C]

oooooooooooooooooooooooooooooooo

THE NAVEL

baby button [1960s+]

belly button [mid-19C+] (orig. US)

innie [1970s+] (an indented navel)

little old man in the boat [late 19C–1900s]

outie [1970s+] (a protruding navel)

salt-cellar [1950s+] (nursery)

THE BUTTOCKS

ampersand [19C] ('&' appeared at the end of 19C nursery alphabets)

back porch [1950s+] (US)

bahakas [1950s+] (US)

bati/batti/batty [1910s+] (W.I.)

booty [1920s+] (US Black)

bottie/botty [mid-19C+]

bum [late 18C+]

bumper [20C] (US)

buns [1960s+]

case o' pistles [20C] (Ulster)

doughy [1950s] (Aus.)

dummock [19C] (Romani, 'behind')

Dutch dumplings [1950s–70s]

parking place

fanny [1920s+] (US)

frances [20C] (US; i.e. 'fanny')

glutes [1980s+] (*glut*eus maximus)

guava [1970s+] (S. Afr.)

heinie [1910s+] (US; *hind* end)

Hottentots [20C] (from the nakedness of African tribespeople)

jutland [19C] (i.e. it *juts* out)

keel [late 19C+]

keister [1930s+] (US; German *Kiste*, a box)

moon [mid-18C+]

naf/naff [mid-19C] (backslang, *fan*, i.e. 'fanny')

Netherlands [18C]

parking place [20C]

patootie/patoot [1920s+] (US)

pooper [1950s+]

prat [16C+]

quoit [1940s+] (Aus.)

rass [1940s+] (W.I.)

roby douglas [late 18C] (a person with 'one eye and stinking breath')

rusty-dusty [1930s–50s] (US)

seat of honour/seat of shame/seat of vengeance [19C]

sitting room [late 19C–1900s]

stern [early 17C+]

thunderbox [20C] (US)

toches [20C] (Yiddish)

tush [late 19C+]

two fat cheeks (and ne'er a nose) [18C]

ultimatum [early 19C]

wazoo [20C] (US)

Westphalia [late 19C–1920s] (punning on *Westphalia* ham, the upper thigh)

○○○○○○○○○○○○○○○○○○○○○○○○○○○○○○○○○○○○○○
The gay backside

cupcakes [1980s+] (US gay)

muffins/English muffins [1960s+] (US gay)

peaches [1980s+] (US gay)

sweetcakes [1980s+] (US gay)

sweetcheeks [1980s+] (US gay)

○○○○○○○○○○○○○○○○○○○○○○○○○○○○○○○○○○○○○○

○○○○○○○○○○○○○○○○○○○○○○○○○○○○○○○○○○○○○○
The buttocks in rhyming slang

Rhyming with 'arse'

aristotle [late 19C+] ('bottle', i.e. 'bottle and glass')

arris [20C] ('*aristotle*')

bottle and glass [20C] (Aus.)

Khyber (Pass) [1940s+]

Rhyming with 'bum'

fife and drum [mid-20C]

kingdom come [1970s]

Tom (Thumb) [20C]

Rhyming with 'tail'

Daily Mail [1930s+]

○○○○○○○○○○○○○○○○○○○○○○○○○○○○○○○○○○○○○○

THE ANUS

arsehole [19C+]

backslice [mid-19C]

barking spider [1980s+]

batcave [1970s–80s]

batty-hole [20C] (W.I.)

○○○○○○○○○○○○○○○○○○○○○○○○○○○○○○○

The anus in rhyming slang

Rhyming with 'arsehole'

elephant and castle [late 19C+]

Windsor castle [20C]

Rhyming with 'shitter'

council gritter [1990s]

Gary Glitter [1990s]

Rhyming with 'jacksie'

London taxi [20C]

Rhyming with 'hole'

merry old soul [20C]

north pole/south pole [20C]

Rhyming with 'ring'

pearly king [20C]

○○○○○○○○○○○○○○○○○○○○○○○○○○○○○○○○○

workman's entrance

brother round mouth [early 19C]

bunghole [17C; 1930s+]

cackpipe [1990s]

camera obscura [late 19C–1900s] (US; Latin, 'dark room')

chute [1970s+] (US)

crack [1960s+]

dirt road [1910s+]

dirt track [1960s+]

dirt-chute [1940s+] (US)

dot [1950s+] (Aus.)

eye of one's arse [20C] (Irish)

flipside [1980s+] (US gay)

flue [20C]

fudge tunnel [1990s]

golden rivet [1940s+]

∘∘∘∘∘∘∘∘∘∘∘∘∘∘∘∘∘∘∘∘∘∘∘∘∘∘∘∘∘∘∘∘∘∘
The anus as a source of excrement

ballinocack [late 18C-early 19C] (Irish; lit. 'shit town')

crapper [1920s+] (orig. US)

dilberry creek [mid–late 19C]

dilberry-maker [mid–late 19C]

dirt box [20C]

dukie hole [1970s+] (US Black; *dukie* = excrement)

fart box [1960s+] (US)

fugo [17C–18C] (*fogo* = the smell of breaking wind)

shit-box [1990s]

shiter [1950s+]

shitter [20C] (US)

spice island [early–mid-19C]

stank [1970s+] (US Black)

stench-trench [20C]

tar pit (US)

winker-stinker [1960s+] (US prison)

∘∘∘∘∘∘∘∘∘∘∘∘∘∘∘∘∘∘∘∘∘∘∘∘∘∘∘∘∘∘∘∘∘∘∘∘

Grand Canyon [1960s+] (US gay)

gripples [20C] (US Black; lit. 'small ditch')

heinie highway [20C] (US; *heinie* = buttocks)

jacksie [late 19C+]

khaki buttonhole [1990s]

Lincoln Tunnel [1960s+] (US gay)

loon pipe [1990s]

monocular eyeglass [mid–late 19C]

mustard pot [1940s–50s]

mustard road [1970s+] (US)

pooh chute [1990s]

poop-chute [20C]

porthole [17C]

ring [late 19C+]

rissole [1970s+] (Aus.; mispron. of 'arsehole')

road less travelled [1990s]

rocky road [20C] (US)

rusty bullet wound [1990s]

shit-chute [20C]

tan track [late 19C+]

tar pit [1970s] (US)

tewel/tuel [late 14C] (lit. 'pipe')

twattling-strings [early 17C–mid-18C] (the anal sphincter, in the context of providing a passageway for wind)

workman's entrance [1990s] (i.e. the 'back door')

°°°°°°°°°°°°°°°°°°°°°°°°°°°°°°°°°°°°°°
Chocolate brown

Bovril bypass [1990s]

brown bullethole [1990s]

Bourneville boulevard [1990s]

Cadbury channel [1990s]

chocolate highway [1970s+] (US)

chocolate runway [1990s]

chocolate starfish [1990s]

chocolate tea-towel holder [1990s]

chocolate whizzway [1990s]

Hershey highway [1970s+] (US)

Marmite motorway [1990s]

old brown windsor [1920s+] (Aus.)

°°°°°°°°°°°°°°°°°°°°°°°°°°°°°°°°°°°°°°

HAEMORRHOIDS

arse-cabbage [1990s]

arse-grapes [1990s]

grapes [1930s–60s] (Aus./US Black)

I.R.S. [1990s+] (*itchy ring syndrome*)

itchy eye [1990s] (US)

Itchypoo Park [1960s]

lilies-of-the-valley [1990s] (gay)

Haemorrhoids in rhyming slang

Rhyming with 'piles'

chalfonts [1970s+] (i.e. *chalfont* st giles)

farmer Giles [1950s] (Aus.)

laughs and smiles [20C] (Aus.)

nautical miles [20C]

Nobby Stiles/Nobbies [1990s]

nurembergs [1940s+] (i.e. *nuremberg* trials)

Plymouth Argyles [20C]

Rockfords [1970s] (i.e. *Rockford* Files)

Seven Dials [1970s+]

Rhyming with 'haemorrhoids'

Emmas [1990s] (i.e. *Emma* Freuds)

Sigmunds [1990s] (i.e. *Sigmund* Freuds)

∘∘∘∘∘∘∘∘∘∘∘∘∘∘∘∘∘∘∘∘∘∘∘∘∘∘∘∘∘∘∘∘∘∘∘∘∘

THE MALE GENITALS

accoutrements [19C+]

arsenal [1990s]

bat and balls [1940s+] (Aus.)

dongs and gongs [20C] (US gay)

family jewels [1960s+]

goodies [1950s+] (orig. US)

lunchbox [1990s]

marriage gear [mid-19C+]

meat and two veg [1990s]

necessaries [20C]

okra and prunes [1980s]

packet [1960s+] (orig. gay)

plumbing [1960s+] (orig. US)

private property [20C]

family jewels

rhubarb [late 19C+]

stock-in-trade [late 19C–1900s]

wedding tackle [1910s+]

THE PENIS

belly ruffian [late 17C–18C]

blue-veined custard chucker [1990s]

cock [early 17C+]

Comrade Wobbly [1990s] (mainly upper-middle class)

cucumber [late 19C+]

cutlass [17C]

dick [late 19C+]

Dr Johnson [19C] (he 'stood up' to anyone)

donger [20C] (Aus.)

drumstick [19C–1900s]

fanny rat [1990s]

Father Abraham [19C]

flesh pencil [1990s]

fuck muscle [1980s+] (US gay)

fuckpole [1990s]

harpoon [20C]

holy poker [mid-19C+]

John Thomas [mid-19C+] (a servant's name, thus one who
    'stands' in the presence of a lady)

joy prong [1910s–70s]

love pump [1980s+] (US)

meat [late 16C–18C; 20C]

member for cockshire [mid-19C]

mud snake [1990s] (US)

one-eyed trouser snake [1960s+] (orig. Aus.)

Percy [1960s+]

pink oboe [1990s]

poperine pear [late 16C]

pork sword [1960s+]

○○○○○○○○○○○○○○○○○○○○○○○○○○○○○○○
The erect penis

chubby [1990s]

cockstand [mid-19C+]

general election [20C] (rhy. sl. 'erection')

guided missile [1970s+] (US black)

hard mouthful [20C]

horn [late 18C+]

mountains of Mourne [20C] (rhy. sl. *horn*)

panhandle [1990s]

prong-on [1960s+]

stiffie [1980s+]

Yasser crack-a-fat [1990s] (US)

○○○○○○○○○○○○○○○○○○○○○○○○○○○○○○○

quimwedge [17C]

rod [20C]

sausage [19C+]

schlong [1930s+] (Yiddish, 'snake')

sensitive truncheon [19C]

sugarstick [late 18C–1900s]

thingummy [late 18C+]

tickle faggot [19C]

tummy banana [1980s+]

weapon [early 11C+]

whore-pipe [late 18C–19C]

wooter [1960s] (US)

zipperfish [1990s]

THE TESTICLES

acorns [1970s] (US)

balls [mid-18+]

Beecham's [late 19C+] (i.e. 'pills')

bollocks [late 18C+]

cannonballs [19C]

Christmas crackers [1970s+] (rhy. sl. 'knackers')

cods [19C+]

conkers [1990s]

Ken Dodds [20C] (rhy. sl. 'cods')

knackers [mid-19C+]

love apples [19C; 1980s+]

love spuds [1990s]

male-mules [16C]

marbles [mid-19C+]

nadgers [1950s+]

nads [1960s+] (orig. US)

nutmegs [late 17C–early 19C]

nuts [mid-19C+]

pebbles [19C]

pills [late 19C+]

plums [20C]

rocks [1940s+]

scalloped potatoes [1960s] (US gay)

swingers [19C]

◦◦◦◦◦◦◦◦◦◦◦◦◦◦◦◦◦◦◦◦◦◦◦◦◦◦◦◦◦◦◦◦◦
The scrotum
ballbasket [1960s+]

bollockbag [1990s]

nadbag [1990s]

nutsack [1970s+] (US)

purse [late17C–18C]

winkybag [1990s]

◦◦◦◦◦◦◦◦◦◦◦◦◦◦◦◦◦◦◦◦◦◦◦◦◦◦◦◦◦◦◦◦◦

twiddle-diddles [late 18C–early 19C]

velvet orbs [1960s] (US gay)

whiblin [early–mid-17C]

yongles [1990s]

THE VAGINA

aphrodisiacal tennis court [17C]

axe wound [1990s]

bearded taco [1950s+] (US)

blate [1990s]

blurt [1990s]

boskage of Venus [19C]

bottomless pit [late 18C–early 19C]

bumshop [mid-19C–1900s]

Cape Horn [19C]

carnal-trap [16C]

chopped liver [20C]

chuff [1940s+] (Aus./UK)

Cock Inn [19C-20C]

cock pit [late 18C–20C]

cream jug [19C]

crown of sense [late 17C]

cunt [mid-15C+]

downy bit [late 19C]

dripping pan [18C]

evening socket [1990s] (the man 'plugs it in' at night)

eye that weeps most when best pleased [19C]

fanny [mid-19C+]

fart-daniel [19C] (lit. 'a sucking pig')

fires of hell [19C]

fleshly part [19C]

front bottom [1990s]

fuckhole [late 19C+]

○○○○○○○○○○○○○○○○○○○○○○○○○○○○○○
Receptacles

bag [late 19C–1930s]

box [1940s+]

bucket [1990s] (a loose or large vagina)

mustard pot [late 19C+]

pigeonhole [late 16C–late 17C]

pink velvet sausage wallet [1990s]

pintlecase [19C] (*pintle* = penis)

poke-hole [late 19C+]

prick-purse [19C]

second hole from the back of the neck [20C]

spunk pot [1990s]

stinkpot [1950s–70s] (US Black)

○○○○○○○○○○○○○○○○○○○○○○○○○○○○○○

fun hatch [1990s]

fur pie [20C]

furry bicycle stand [1990s]

gallimaufry [19C] (lit. 'a mess of food')

gash [18C+]

golden doughnut [20C]

gorilla burger [1990s]

grommet [late 19C–1940s] (US)

Hairyfordshire [mid-19C]

hey-nonny-no [late 16C–mid-18C]

holy Dorito [1990s]

hypogastrian cranny [mid-17C] (Greek *hypograstrium*, that part of the body below the belly and above the privates)

inglenook [19C]

○○○○○○○○○○○○○○○○○○○○○○○○○○○○○○○
Marine life
bearded oyster [1910s+]

fuzzy lap flounder [1990s]

cod trench [1990s]

haddock pastie [1990s]

hirsute oyster [1990s]

red snapper [20C] (US)

snapping turtle [20C]

○○○○○○○○○○○○○○○○○○○○○○○○○○○○○○○

The vagina in rhyming slang

Rhyming with 'cunt'

Berkeley hunt [1930s+]

Burlington hunt [1930s+]

gasp and grunt [1930s+]

sharp and blunt [20C]

Sir Berkeley [1930s] (i.e. *Berkeley* hunt)

Rhyming with 'fanny'

Jack an' Danny [1990s]

Rhyming with 'gash'

Leslie [1990s] (i.e. *Leslie* Ash)

kazoo [1960s+]

leather [mid-16C+]

love canal [1980s+] (US)

love glove [1980s+] (US)

main vein [1950s+]

mangle [19C]

Mickey Mouse [1930s–40s] (US)

milt shop [19C] (*milt* = roe)

minge [20C]

Miss Laycock [late 18C–early 19C]

mossy cottage [1990s]

mossy doughnut [1940s] (US)

nanty crackling [late 19C–1920s]

nature's tufted treasure [19C]

nether eye [19C]

nookie [1960s+] (orig. US)

old frizzle [18C–late 19C]

old lady [mid-19C+]

P.E.E.P. [1980s+] (US; '*p*erfectly *e*xcellent *e*ating *p*ussy')

parking lot [1960s–70s] (US)

part of India [late 16C–early 17C] (from the shape of the pudendum)

poontang [1920s+] (orig. US; French *putain*, a whore)

quim [early 18C+] (Welsh *cwm*, a valley)

serpent socket [1990s]

snatch [late 19C+]

South Pole [19C]

standing room for one [19C]

thatched house under the hill [19C]

tickle Thomas [19C]

trench [19C]

twange [1990s]

twat [mid-17C+] (dial. *twitchel*, 'a narrow passage')

under-dimple [19C]

where the monkey sleeps

velvet tunnel [1990s]

vertical smile [20C]

where the monkey sleeps [20C]

THE LEG(S)

baccy stick [late 19C] (US)

bender [mid-19C+]

board [1960s] (US)

cabbage stumps [19C]

chalks [mid-19C]

drivers [1970s] (US campus)

drumsticks [mid-19C+]

flippers [late 19C+] (US)

get-along [20C] (US)

ham-hocks [1930s–40s] (US Black; female legs or ankles)

hind paw [1920s]

lallie/lallette/lally/lyle [1950s+] (Ling. Fr./Polari)

locomotives [mid-19C]

nag [late 18C]

pair of compasses [late 19C]

pegs [mid-19C+]

pestle of pork [late 19C–1900s]

●●●●●●●●●●●●●●●●●●●●●●●●●●●●●●●
The legs in rhyming slang

bacon and eggs [1950s+] (orig. Aus.)

clothes-pegs [20C]

cribbage-pegs [1920s]

Dutch pegs [20C]

fried eggs [20C] (Aus.)

gregory pegs [20C] (Aus.)

ham and eggs [1950s+] (orig. Aus.)

mumbly pegs [1920s–40s]

Scotch (egg) [mid-19C+]

Scotch pegs [mid-19C+]

scrambled eggs [20C]

●●●●●●●●●●●●●●●●●●●●●●●●●●●●●●●●●

pillars [1930s]

pins [mid-19C+]

pods [19C] (children's legs)

props [late 18C–late 19C; 1950s–60s] (attractive female legs)

rammer [late 18C–19C]

scotchie [late 19C–1930s]

shafts [1930s–40s]

skiff [late 19C–1900s]

spindle [19C]

stalks [1960s]

stamps [mid-16C–late 18C]

stems [mid-19C+] (attractive female legs)

sticks [early–mid-19C]

stilts [1940s]

stumps [early 18C]

taxi eleven [1950s+]

timbers [18C–mid-19C]

toddlers [mid-19C]

trams [20C]

trespassers [19C]

twigs [1930s–40s]

underpinners [mid-19C] (US)

underpinnings [mid-19C+]

understandings [early–mid-19C]

wheels [1950s+]

○○○○○○○○○○○○○○○○○○○○○○○○○○○○○○○○○○○
Fat, thin and other unsightly legs

badger-legged [mid-17C–early 18C] (having legs of unequal length)

beef to the heel (like a Mullingar heifer) [mid-19C+] (thick, bulky legs or ankles)

beefy [mid-19C+] (thick ankled)

bottle legs [20C] (crooked legs)

buckle-hammed [early 17C] (having crooked legs)

cat sticks [late 18C–19C] (very thin legs)

cheese-cutters [mid-19C] (bandy legs)

cow-hocked/double-hocked [mid–late 19C] (thick ankled)

gummy [mid-18C–mid-19C] (thick ankled)

Irish arms [20C] (thick legs)

pudding about the heels [late 19C–1900s] (thick ankles)

spiddock-pot legs [17C] (ungainly legs)

tampon braces [1930s–40s] (US Black; unattractive female legs)

trapsticks [early 18C–mid-19C] (thin legs)

○○○○○○○○○○○○○○○○○○○○○○○○○○○○○○○○○○○

THE KNEES

benders [mid-19C+]

capital K [1940s+] (W.I.; knock-knees)

deuce of benders [1930s–40s] (US Black/Harlem)

hambones [1900s] (US)

k-foot [1940s+] (knock-knees)

knobs [1940s+]

marrowbones [mid-16C–1900s]

prayer-bones [late 19C–1940s] (US Black)

○○○○○○○○○○○○○○○○○○○○○○○○○○○○○○○○
The knees in rhyming slang
biscuits and cheese [1940s+]

bread and cheese [late 19C+]

bugs and fleas [1940s] (US)

Robert E. Lees [20C]

○○○○○○○○○○○○○○○○○○○○○○○○○○○○○○○○

THE FEET

ards [17C] (UK Und.)

beetle-crusher [mid-19C+]

beetle-squasher [mid-19C]

boot-trees [19C]

chockers [late 19C+] (market trader)

crabs [late 18C–1910s]

creepers [19C+]

creeps [20C] (US Black)

crunchers [1940s] (US)

daisy-beaters [late 19C+]

dancers [mid-17C–mid-19C]

dew-beaters [late 18C–late 19C] (UK Und.)

dew-dusters/dew-treaders [19C]

dog-kickers [mid-19C] (US)

earth pads [1940s]

everlasting shoes [mid-19C]

fives [17C]

frog [late 19C–1900s]

○○○○○○○○○○○○○○○○○○○○○○○○○○○○○○○○○○
Flat feet and club feet

brace of horned cows [late 19C–1940s] (US Black; a pair of aching feet)

double-breasters [19C] (club feet)

hurley foot [20C] (a club-foot)

gut food [1930s–40s] (US Black; fallen arches, i.e. flat feet)

palmer houses [1930s–40s] (flat feet)

○○○○○○○○○○○○○○○○○○○○○○○○○○○○○○○○○○

puppies

goers [19C]

groundpads/groundbags [1930s–40s]

hind paw [1920s]

hind-shifters [mid-19C]

hocks [mid-19C]

hoof [late 16C+]

kickers [mid-19C+]

mud-masher [mid-19C+]

mud pads [1910s–20s]

mud scows [early 19C–1910s] (lit. 'mud boats')

○○○○○○○○○○○○○○○○○○○○○○○○○○○○○○○○○○○○○○
The feet in rhyming slang

dogs [1920s+] (i.e. *dog's* meat)

gillie potters [1950s+] ('trotters')

plates (of meat) [late 19C+]

platters (of meat) [1920s]

○○○○○○○○○○○○○○○○○○○○○○○○○○○○○○○○○○○○○○

○○○○○○○○○○○○○○○○○○○○○○○○○○○○○○○○○○○○○○
Large feet

airy-fairies [1930s]

ant-killer [mid-19C]

ant-stomper [1970s]

barge [1950s+] (US)

boat [1950s+] (US)

boxcar [1950s–70s] (US)

canal boat [20C] (US)

clodhopper [18C+]

club-foot [20C] (US)

curby hocks [mid-19C–1900s]

flannel feet [20C]

flapper [20C] (US)

forty acres [20C] (US)

mud flaps [1950s+]

shipyards [20C]

○○○○○○○○○○○○○○○○○○○○○○○○○○○○○○○○○○○○○○

padders [19C]

pedestals [early 18C]

pettitoes [early 18C]

plonkers [1920s+]

pudseys [late 18C+]

puppies [1910s+]

stamps [mid-16C–late 18C]

steppers [mid-19C]

toddlers [early–mid-19C]

tootsies [mid-19C+]

trampers [19C]

trods [1940s]

trotters [late 17C+]

walkers [early 17C–early 19C]

THE TOES

buttons and bows [20C] (Aus.; rhy. sl.)

council-of-ten [mid-19C] (pigeon toes)

old black joes [20C] (rhy. sl.)

scratcher [19C]

stop and go [20C] (rhy. sl.)

ten [1940s]

these and those [20C] (rhy. sl.)